Translation, History and Culture

Translation, History and Culture

Edited by
Susan Bassnett and André Lefevere

Pinter Publishers
London and New York

© Susan Bassnett and André Lefevere 1990

First published in Great Britain in 1990 by
Pinter Publishers Limited
25 Floral Street, London WC2E 9DS

British Library Cataloguing in Publication Data

A CIP catalogue record for this book is available from the
British Library
ISBN 0-86187-100-6

Library of Congress Cataloguing in Publication Data

Translation, history, and culture / edited by Susan Bassnett and André Lefevere.
     p.   cm.
  ISBN 0-86187-100-6
  1. Translating and interpreting.   2. Language and culture.
  I. Bassnett, Susan.   II. Lefevere, André.
  P306.T735   1990
  418'.02--dc20   90-32054
                                                                          CIP

Typeset by Acorn Bookwork, Salisbury, Wiltshire
Printed and bound in Great Britain by Biddles Ltd, of Guildford and Kings Lynn

Contents

List of contributors

Susan Bassnett is Reader and head of the Graduate School of Comparative Literary Theory and Translation Studies at the University of Warwick. Her books include *Translation Studies* (Methuen/Routledge 1980/90), *Feminist Experiences: The Women's Movement in Four Cultures* (Allen and Unwin, 1986) and works on theatre history, comparative literature, women's writing and Latin American literature. She is a poet and translator and has four children.

Dirk Delabastita is a research assistant in the Dept of English, Université de la Paix, Namur, Belgium. He is co-editor with H. Van Gorp of *Lexicon van Literaire Termen* (1986) and is currently completing his doctoral dissertation on the translation of Shakespearian wordplay.

Barbara Godard is Associate Professor of English at York University, Ontario. She has published widely on Canadian and Quebec writers and on feminist critical theory. A translator, she has presented Quebec women writers Louky Bersianik, Yolande Villemaire and Antonine Maillet to an English audience. Her translation of Brossard's *Picture Theory* will appear in 1991.

Mette Hjort is an Assistant Professor in the Dept of English at McGill University. She is the translator of Louis Marin's *Food For Thought* (The Johns Hopkins University Press, 1989) and has published on the Frankfurt School and on Antitheatricality in England and France.

Piotr Kuhiwczak is Honorary Fellow in the Graduate School of Comparative Literary Theory and Translation Studies at the University of Warwick and teaches English literature at the University of Warsaw. He has published studies of Romantic poetry and has translated into Polish and into English.

André Lefevere is Professor in the Dept of Germanic Languages, University of Texas at Austin and Honorary Professor of Translation Studies at the University of Warwick. He is the author of several books and numerous articles on translation theory, genre theory and literary theory which he believes to be intimately related. He is also a translator of Dutch, German and French literature into English.

Vladimír Macura is a research scholar in the Institute for the study of Czech and World Literature in the Czechoslovak Academy of Sciences in Prague. He has published in the field of semiotics of culture, poetics and theory of literature. Since 1978 he has translated some 20 books from Esthonian into Czech.

Mahasweta Sengupta holds a PhD in English Literature and taught at Visva Bharati University, Santiniketan, India before joining the Dept of Comparative Literature, University of Massachusetts, Amherst, where she is writing a doctoral dissertation on the cross-cultural implications of the translations of Tagore read in the context of post-colonial criticism.

Sherry Simon teaches in the French Dept. at Concordia University, Montreal. She is co-editor of *Spirale*, a Quebec cultural review and is active in the Canadian Literary Translators Association. With David Homel, she edited *Mapping Literature: The Art and Politics of Translation* (Vehicule Press, 1988) and has recently published *L'inscription sociale de la traduction au Québec* (Office de la langue française, Gouvernement de Québec).

Mary Snell-Hornby is Professor of Translation at the University of Vienna. She is well-known for her work in Translation Studies and has held Chairs in several German, Swiss and Austrian universities before taking up her present post.

Elzbieta Tabakowska is Associate Professor in the Institute of English at the Jagellonian University of Krakow, Poland. Her research interests are theoretical and practical problems involved in interlingual literary translation. She has published articles on contrastive linguistics and translation, and a large number of translations from English into Polish.

Maria Tymoczko received her PhD in Celtic and Romance Languages and Literatures from Harvard University. She is Professor of Comparative Literature at the University of Massachusetts, Amherst where she specializes in medieval literature, Irish literature and Translation Studies.

Palma Zlateva is a researcher in the Translation Theory section of the Bulgarian Language Institute at the Bulgarian Academy of Sciences. She also teaches English-Bulgarian translation in the Dept of English at the Unviersity of Sofia. She holds a PhD from the M. Thorez Foreign Languages Institute in Moscow. She has published extensively in the field of Translation Studies.

Preface

The growth of Translation Studies as a separate discipline is a success story of the 1980s. The subject has developed in many parts of the world and is clearly destined to continue developing well into the 21st century. Translation studies brings together work in a wide variety of fields, including linguistics, literary study, history, anthropology, psychology and economics. This series of books will reflect the breadth of work in Translation Studies and will enable readers to share in the exciting new developments that are taking place at the present time.

Translation is, of course, a rewriting of an original text. All rewritings, whatever their intention, reflect a certain ideology and a poetics and as such manipulate literature to function in a given society in a given way. Rewriting is manipulation, undertaken in the service of power, and in its positive aspect can help in the evolution of a literature and a society. Rewritings can introduce new concepts, new genres, new devices and the history of translation is the history also of literary innovation, of the shaping power of one culture upon another. But rewriting can also repress innovation, distort and contain, and in an age of ever increasing manipulation of all kinds, the study of the manipulative processes of literature as exemplified by transltaion can help us towards a greater awareness of the world in which we live.

Since this series of books on Translation Studies is the first of its kind, it will be concerned with its own genealogy. It will publish texts from the past that illustrate its concerns in the present, and will publish texts of a more theoretical nature immediately addressing those concerns, along with case studies illustrating manipulation through rewriting in various literatures. It will be comparative in nature and will range through many literary traditions both Western and non-Western. Through the concepts of rewriting and manipulation, this series aims to tackle the problem of ideology, change and power in literature and society and so assert the central function of translation as a shaping force.

Susan Bassnett
André Lefevere
1990

Introduction: Proust's Grandmother and the Thousand and One Nights: The 'Cultural Turn' in Translation Studies

André Lefevere and Susan Bassnett

In *Sodome et Gomorrhe* Marcel Proust's narrator muses about his grandmother's attitude towards translations and, more especially, new translations superseding the translations she has been familiar with all her life. To put it briefly, she does not like them at all. The reasons why will provide a useful starting point for the introduction to a volume of essays trying to rethink the role of translation in literary studies in a way that finally begins to do justice to the central role translation has played in Western culture almost from the very beginning.

But first, the grandmother:

If an *Odyssey* from which the names of Ulysses and Minerva were absent was no longer the *Odyssey* for her, what would she have said when she saw the title of her *Thousand and One Nights* already deformed on the title page, when she could no longer find the immortally familiar names of Sheherazade and Dinarazade transcribed exactly as she had been used to pronouncing them from time immemorial in a book where the charming Caliph and the powerful Genies were hardly able to recognize themselves, having been decapitated as it were, if one dares use that word in the context of Muslim stories, and now being called one the 'Khalifat', the others the 'Gennis?' (Proust, 1954: 238–9; trans. A. Lefevere).

The text quoted immediately directs our attention to a number of points, few of which, if any, will be made by authors of linguistic studies of translation.

The first point is that the grandmother quite obviously accepts the existence of translations as such. It is unlikely that she will have read either the *Odyssey* or *The Thousand and One Nights*, or both, in the original. Unlike a certain group of theoreticians of translation, therefore, discussed in Mette Hjort's contribution to this volume, Proust's grandmother definitely thinks translation is possible. We might even go on to surmise that, like many of her contemporaries and many who have lived in successive generations since, she may never have been very interested in the problem as such. Her initial attitude towards translations can, therefore, be said to have been of a somewhat pragmatic nature: since they exist, let us make use of them.

Yet Proust's grandmother clearly distinguishes between what are, to her, 'good' and 'bad' translations. It should be noted, however, that 'good' and 'bad' have, for her, no bearing whatsoever on the actual 'quality' of the translations, since that is precisely a feature of translation she is utterly unable to judge. Rather, Proust's grandmother likes the translations she has grown up with. 'The' *Odyssey* for her is a translation in which the hero is still called by his Latinized name: Ulysses, and in which the goddess Athena is likewise still called Minerva. Other *Odysseys* or rather, other texts deemed to represent Homer's *Odyssey*, simply will not do, they are impostors, as are translations of *The Thousand and One Nights* that change the very names of the protagonists.

Proust's grandmother, therefore, does not really like or dislike a translation; rather, she trusts or distrusts a translator. The translator whose work she is familiar with is, to her, a 'faithful' translator. Of course Proust's grandmother is not the only person to determine whether a translation is 'faithful' or not. It is highly unlikely, for instance, that the publisher of the translations Proust's grandmother liked published them solely because he liked them. Then, as now, he will most probably have had the translation read by a number of 'experts' in the field, and he will have published the translation at least in part because of their favourable recommendation.

Yet, suddenly, a translation appears in which the 'immortally familiar' Ulysses has been transmogrified into the barbaric Odysseus, and another translation in which the beloved 'Caliph' has been mutilated almost beyond all recognition and is now called 'Khalifat'. What has gone wrong? Why was it necessary to publish new translations designed at least to compete with the familiar old translations, or even to supersede them altogether? Were the experts wrong? Did they change their minds? If they did, who can we ever trust again?

Something has, indeed, changed between two translations, but that something was not any expert's mind. Rather, the experts who gave the translations familiar to Proust's grandmother a favourable recommendation have, most likely, passed on and been replaced by other experts. But surely we are entitled to ask, together with Proust's grandmother, that should not matter, because are the standards themselves not for ever beyond any conceivable change?

Proust's grandmother finds herself in distinguished company here, namely that of many more linguistically oriented writers on translation who, as Mary Snell-Hornby points out in her chapter, cling rather tenaciously to standards of that nature: 'equivalence' was (and is) one such, second only to the admittedly somewhat chimerical, but therefore all the more inexorable *tertium comparationis*, the 'something' which presumably hovers somewhere between languages in some kind of air bubble and 'guarantees' (no less) that a word in the language you translate into (target language) is, indeed, equivalent to a word in the language you translate from (source language). The celebrated *tertium comparationis* would, therefore, guarantee that your translation say: 'Le baisage du dernier ménestrel' is equivalent to the title of Sir Walter Scott's original *Lay of the Last Minstrel*, were it not for the unfortunate fact that the primary meaning of 'lay' has shifted somewhat in English over the last 180 years.

The trouble with standards, it would seem, is that they turn out not to be eternal and unchanging after all. Most writers on translation who come to the subject from linguistics appear to be unable to face this, probably because they are (still) caught up in the more positivistic aspects of linguistics – what Snell-Hornby calls its 'scientistic' side. And positivism, which was beginning to dominate science at the time of Proust's grandmother, was bent, among other things, on casting out relativity, on which a paper which would prove to be rather influential was published sixteen years before the eventual publication of *Sodome et Gomorrhe* itself. And yet, though many linguists writing on translation have no doubt familiarized themselves with the work of Sir Karl Popper, Thomas Kuhn and other theorists of science, positivism still leads a shadowy existence as the 'invisible theory' (Livingston, 1988: 13) behind much of what those same linguists write on our topic.

The *tertium comparationis* raises more problems – more, in the end, than it is worth, but we shall only list one more here – suppose it 'guarantees' that every word used in a translation is 'equivalent' to every word used in the original. There is no way it can 'guarantee' that the translation will have an effect on readers belonging to the target culture which is in any way comparable to the effect the original may have had on readers belonging to the source culture. Every word in the Loeb Classical Library's translation of the *Odyssey*, for instance, is no doubt equivalent to every word in Homer's original. The original is literature, the translation a crib. Or take the case of Emile Littré's celebrated translation of Dante's *Divina Commedia* into thirteenth-century French. Again, every word in the translation is equivalent to every word in the original, but very few readers of the translation would have been able to understand it any better than the original.

Those who write on the linguistic aspects of translation will, no doubt, think the above comments unfair. They began to write about translation the way they did not necessarily because of any deep 'scientific' conviction, but because the fifties of this century were the time when many in the field were either convinced, or very willing to let themselves be convinced, that the triumph of machine translation was just around the corner. And machines need to be programmed, and well programmed. Hence the emphasis on equivalence and 'guarantees', and the focus, almost exclusively for a long time, on the word as the unit of translation. Later linguists have moved from word to text as a unit, but not beyond. Furthermore, they would argue that what they have written on translation was never meant to be applied to the translation of literature, since literature, the argument went, was 'a special case'. It is not clear whether we are to understand by this that literature is not really written in any language at all, or in a language so different from the language linguists would like to analyse that it is not worth the effort. The overall position of the linguist in translation studies would be rather analogous to that of an intrepid explorer who refuses to take any notice of the trees in the new region he has discovered until he has made sure he has painstakingly arrived at a description of all the plants that grow there.

At the end of her contribution, Mary Snell-Hornby exhorts linguists to abandon their 'scientistic' attitude and to move from 'text' as a putative 'translation unit', to culture – a momentous step that would go far beyond the move from the word as a 'unit' to the text. The contributions in this volume have all taken the 'cultural turn' advocated by Snell-Hornby, which explains why certain staple features characterizing 'volumes of essays on translation' as published in the past will no longer be found here, and why certain new categories – new, at least, in comparison to volumes of the kind just mentioned – will be introduced. The 'cultural turn' also explains why this volume, as opposed to so many others in the field, displays a remarkable unity of purpose. All contributions deal with the 'cultural turn' in one way or another, they are so many case studies illustrating the central concept of the collection.

The reader will no longer find painstaking comparisons between originals and translations, largely because such comparisons, after paying lip service to the text-as-unit, tend to fall victim to the 'invisible theory' of the *tertium comparationis* which is implicitly postulated to underwrite judgements on why a certain translation (usually the one proposed by the writer of the paper in question) is better than another (usually contained in the translation being compared with its original). Nor will the reader find suggestions for either the production of foolproof translations or the training of foolproof translators, simply because both are utopian chimerae, to say the least.

Two contributions in the present volume touch on the one feature that makes the 'cultural turn' all but inevitable: time or, if you prefer, history. Over and against the positivistically posited existence of absolute standards by which a translation should be measured – standards so absolute that any text presenting itself as a translation would be found wanting – Mette Hjort argues that texts presenting themselves as translations of other texts can and do satisfy appropriateness conditions and intersubjectively mediated rules and norms dominant in the field of translation in a certain culture at a certain time. For most of the nineteenth century, for instance, one of the appropriateness conditions to be satisfied in the translation of poetry was that the translation had to rhyme – even if, as in the case of the Greek and Roman classics, the original did not. One of the 'norms' mediated in that century in connection with translations of those classics was that they needed to be kept on the 'classical' level: erotic and scatological passages would either not be translated or, in the case of the Loeb Classical Library, translated from Greek into Latin and from Latin into Italian. (It is hardly a coincidence, therefore, that Latin and Italian dictionaries tend to suffer most from use in public libraries in the British Isles.)

Mette Hjort states that norms, rules and appropriateness conditions are liable to change. Translations made at different times therefore tend to be made under different conditions and to turn out differently, not because they are good or bad, but because they have been produced to satisfy different demands. It cannot be stressed enough that the production of different translations at different times does not point to any 'betrayal' of absolute standards, but rather to the absence, pure and simple, of any such standards. Such are the facts of life in the production – and study – of translations.

André Lefevere attempts a sketch of a genealogy of translation in the West, both documenting the changes in question and trying to explain why they occurred. Empirical historical research can document the changes he lists; to explain them, he needs to go into the vagaries and vicissitudes of the exercise of power in a society, and what the exercise of power means in terms of the production of culture, of which the production of translations is a part. The 'invisible presence' behind much of his writing is, of course, that of Michel Foucault. It should be noted here, too, that the concepts of norms and rules, which have already been mentioned, as well as the concept of the function of the translated text, which will soon be brought into play, were introduced nearly a decade ago by the Israeli translation scholar Gideon Toury. Yet his somewhat more than hermetic style, as well as the relative inaccessibility of his book, owing partially to the relative obscurity of its publisher, have tended to obstruct, rather than facilitate the spread of his ideas.

Both Barbara Godard and Mahasweta Sengupta deal with the category of power as a constraint on the production of translations. Barbara Godard documents how feminist writing uses translation to subvert dominant (male) discourse. In doing so, she links translation 'proper' to parody, thus pointing out one more direction in which the field of translation studies can grow. In his contribution, Dirk Delabastita points out yet another, complementary direction; we shall come back to both near the end of this introduction. In the body of her text Godard decisively eliminates 'equivalence' as the precondition, or even the goal, of translation. Rather translation should amount to 'transformation', a term which appears to be the other side of Piotr Kuhiwczak's 'appropriation'.

In both cases we are faced with texts purporting to be 'translations' of a source text, yet in both cases the translators wittingly and willingly manipulate the source text to make it serve their own ends. The feminist writers Godard mentions manipulate with the aim of advancing their own ideology. The translators Kuhiwczak mentions manipulate mainly to protect the reader not from an ideology (Kundera is not suspect in *that* respect, anyway) but from a poetics: Kundera writes novels in such a way that they may be too difficult for the average English-speaking reader to understand, and they must therefore be simplified, be made to read more like what that average reader (whoever s/he may be) is used to. Kuhiwczak's case study is also a perfect illustration of the use of power in Foucault's sense, which is also the sense in which 'power' is to be understood in this introduction. Foucault writes:

If power were never anything but repressive, if it never did anything but to say no, do you really think one would be brought to obey it? What makes power hold good, what makes it accepted, is simply the fact that it doesn't only weigh on us as a force that says no, but that it traverses and produces things, it induces pleasure, forms knowledge, produces discourse. (1980: 119)

The publisher who allows the translators to manipulate/mutilate the original does, at the same time, have the power to introduce Kundera to a new audience, albeit not in optimal conditions. And the conditions are not optimal because the publisher has to bow to another kind of power, that wielded by his banker(s): he will not be able to publish anything any more in the not too distant future if what he publishes now does not sell.

Translation as mimicry of the dominant discourse (i.e. the discourse of the colonizer) is the topic of Mahasweta Sengupta's contribution on Rabindranath Tagore's auto-translations. She convincingly demonstrates that Tagore wrote in a totally different style in English and in Bengali, and that his fame in England, Europe and the Americas was severely limited by the way he could be made to function within the structure of imperial power: as long as he accepted the role of the sage, or even mystic imposed on him, he was *also* hailed as a great poet. Once he began to lecture against nationalism during the First World War, his star began to wane in England and its dominions.

This, then, is perhaps the time to introduce the category of 'function' in translation studies. It is obvious that not everyone in the field will be happy with a notion of translation that encompasses both an interlinear version of a poem, say, *and* the cases of 'transformation', of 'appropriation', and of 'mimicry' described earlier. Translations are never produced in an airlock where they, and their originals, can be checked against the *tertium comparationis* in the purest possible lexical chamber, untainted by power, time, or even the vagaries of culture. Rather, translations are made to respond to the demands of a culture, and of various groups within that culture. This is probably never more clearly in evidence than when two cultures live together within the borders of one state, as evidenced by Sherry Simon's analysis of French/English translations, and vice versa, in Canada.

Cultures make various demands on translations, and those demands also have to do with the status of the text to be translated. If the text comes even close to the status of 'metanarrative' (Lyotard, 1985: xxxiv), or 'central text' embodying the fundamental beliefs of a culture (the Bible, the Koran), chances are the culture will demand the most literal translation possible. The same will generally hold true of scientific and technical texts: even if a computer manual has been written by a man, no woman translator is likely to get away with a translation that 'subverts male discourse' to such an extent that users begin to return the machines because they cannot figure out how to operate them. If, on the other hand, the text has little, or acceptably little, to do with either the beliefs of members of a culture, or their bank accounts, as is the case with most literary texts, translators are likely to be given much more leeway.

Proust's grandmother liked a translation of the *Odyssey* in which the hero was called 'Ulysses'. Yet a professor of classics occasionally visiting her 'salon' might have far preferred a translation restoring to the hero his original name of 'Odysseus'. Neither preference is likely to have caused the collapse of the political and/or financial institutions of the French Third Republic. Both Proust's grandmother and our fictitious professor of classics might also have concurred in the opinion that if a children's version of the *Odyssey* were to appear in the 'Bibliothèque Bleue', or some other series aimed at children, it should probably not contain every single part of the action of the original.

'Faithfulness', then, does not enter into translation in the guise of 'equivalence' between words or texts but, if at all, in the guise of an attempt to make the target text function in the target culture the way the source text functioned in the source culture. Translations are therefore not 'faithful' on the levels they have traditionally been required to be – to achieve 'functional equivalence' a translator may have to substantially adapt the source text. Translators, on the other hand, can be faithful, and they are said to be when they deliver what those who commission their translations want: 'Ulysses', among other features, for Proust's grandmother; 'Odysseus', among other features, for her acquaintance the classics professor.

A culture, then, assigns different functions to translations of different texts. The way translations are supposed to function depends both on the audience they are intended for (there are very few translations of *Gulliver's Travels* for children, for instance, in which the hero actually urinates on the imperial palace of Lilliput to put out the flames that threaten to consume it, as he does in the original – he usually runs to the sea, fills his hat with water and empties it over the palace), and on the status of the source text they are supposed to represent in their own culture. In some cases, one of which has been described in this volume by Vladimír Macura, translation actually 'constitutes' a culture. In his contribution, Macura shows how nineteenth-century Czech culture virtually 'cloned' itself on the German model. In this case the 'function' of translation has very little to do with the transfer of information which is so often claimed to be its one and only *raison d'être*, since, as Macura points out, the readers of the translation did not really need it at all, as they were perfectly able to read the original. Translation, then, becomes one of the means by which a new nation 'proves' itself, shows that its language is capable of rendering what is rendered in more prestigious languages – as when Julius Nyerere, for instance, translates Shakespeare into Swahili. Translation, in this case, amounts to a seizure of power, more than anything else, any transfer of anything at all.

If neither the word, nor the text, but the culture becomes the operational 'unit' of translation, it might be wise to distinguish between 'intracultural' and 'intercultural' translation, even though it is doubtful whether these kinds of distinctions and definitions are likely to be blessed with a long life. Let us try to put it this way: in every culture there are texts which claim to represent other texts. Some of these texts claim to represent texts belonging to a different culture; they are usually known as 'translations'. Proust's grandmother, for instance, read a book called *The Thousand and One Nights*, which represented for her a book written originally in Arabic which she was unable to read. Yet some of these texts also claim to represent texts belonging to the same culture. Excerpts from the work of

Proust's grandmother's grandson, for instance, or Marcel himself, if you prefer, tend to appear in school and university anthologies in France. Professors and other scholars write critical essays on *Sodome et Gomorrhe* and other volumes of *Á la recherche du temps perdu* in French, and publish them as books or in French scholarly journals. Histories of French literature, published in Paris, Quebec or Dakar are likely to include at least some attempt at a summary of *Á la recherche*, and there are professors busily writing almost line-by-line commentaries, designed to elucidate nearly every word. But the French-speaking man or woman in the street is likely to think of Jeremy Irons when asked about Swann, if s/he thinks of anything or anybody at all. The movie based on *Un amour de Swann* is likely to have represented Proust to many more people than any of the other forms of representation described here. This, then, would be the 'intracultural' translation, which we propose to call 'rewriting', with the proviso that certain texts originally translated from another culture (the Bible, Lenin, Shakespeare) can become naturalized to such an extent that they are given the same 'intracultural' treatment as texts which have originally been generated within the culture in question.

Now let us turn the argument around, and look at it from the receiving end. It is extremely unlikely that the great majority of French-speaking people have actually ploughed through the whole of *Á la recherche*. Yet they will all 'have read' or at least 'know' Proust. If they have read him, chances are they have read short excerpts in anthologies; if they 'know' him and they are professional students of literature, they may have read one or two volumes of *Á la recherche* and supplemented this 'basic' knowledge with further knowledge gleaned from criticism, histories and commentaries, often during those dark nights of the soul preceding final examinations. If they are not professional students of literature, they will feel they can, at all times, look up 'Proust' in the *Petit Larousse* and, if all else fails, they can claim to have seen the movie.

We suggest that this is cultural reality, i.e. this is the way literature operates in a culture in this day and age. Since 'our common culture, however much we might wish it were not so, is less and less a book culture and more and more a culture of cinema, television and popular music' (Hillis Miller, 1987: 285), literature reaches those who are not its professional students much more by way of the 'images' constructed of it in translations, but even more so in anthologies, commentaries, histories and, occasionally, critical journals, than it does so by means of 'originals', however venerable they may be, and however much professors of literature and its students who approach it in a 'professional' way may regret this state of affairs. What impacts most on members of a culture, we suggest, is the 'image' of a work of literature, not its 'reality', not the text that is still sacrosanct only in literature departments. It is therefore extremely important that the 'image' of a literature and the works that constitute it be studied alongside its reality. This, we submit, is where the future of 'translation studies' lies.

'Translation', then, is one of the many forms in which works of literature are 'rewritten', one of many 'rewritings'. In our day and age, these 'rewritings' are at least as influential in ensuring the survival of a work of literature as the originals, the 'writings' themselves. One might even take the next step and say that if a work is not 'rewritten' in one way or another, it is not likely to survive its publication date by all that many years, or even months. Needless to say, this state of affairs invests a non-negligible power in the rewriters: translators, critics, historians, professors, journalists. They can make or break a writer, and they can – as the Kundera example shows – make and break him or her on their own terms. Their power should, therefore, be analysed, as well as the various ways in which they tend to exercise it.

If we study rewritings of all kinds: translations, histories, critical articles, commentaries, anthologies, anything that contributes to constructing the 'image' of a writer and/or a work of literature, there is, as Dirk Delabastita reminds us, no reason why we should stop at rewritings in the written medium as we usually understand it. His contribution to this volume takes the whole concept one step further, into the 'rewriting' of film, arguably the most powerful medium today. His contribution could be said to represent one pole of a future 'translation/rewriting studies'. The other pole could be represented by the contributions by Palma Zlateva and Elzbieta Tabakowska appearing in this volume. Whereas Delabastita deals with a more 'global' picture, both Zlateva and Tabakowska engage in what could be called detail studies by comparison, but the difference between their detail studies and those contained in 'volumes of essays on translation' published in the past should be obvious. Zlateva's concept of 'pre-text', i.e. the cultural assumptions that largely determine the success or failure of a translated text in the target culture, and which have almost nothing to do with the quality of the translation itself, seems destined for a fruitful career in translation/rewriting studies, if only because publishers, as described by Kuhiwczak, often use the pre-text problem as a pretext not even to consider a translation for publication. Finally, Tabakowska demonstrates the extent to which culture 'shows' in both text and translation. The original, she argues, is not a monolithic statement made by one speaker, which should therefore be translated in the same monolithic manner. Rather, the source text is already a polyphonic statement, and the translation should inspire similar, or at least analogous, polyphonic reactions in its readers. We have come far indeed from a certain concept of equivalence which held, in practice, that anybody with a fairly good knowledge of two languages supplemented by a fairly reliable dictionary, should be able to produce fairly decent translations. Since languages express cultures, translators should be bicultural, not bilingual.

What the development of Translation Studies shows is that translation, like all (re)writings is never innocent. There is always a context in which the translation takes place, always a history from which a text emerges and into which a text is transposed. Translation involves so much more than the simple engagement of an individual with a printed page and a bilingual dictionary; indeed, the bilingual dictionary itself is an object lesson in the inadequacy of any concept of equivalence as linguistic sameness. How many readers are constantly frustrated as they endeavour to look up a word or phrase in a bilingual dictionary, only to discover that the range of terms available offers them a series of choices that they are ill-equipped to undertake. Examples of the kind of translation that results from blind trust in a bilingual dictionary divorced from contextual knowledge abound; wherever one travels one encounters tourist brochures, hotel information documents, instructions in elevators and so forth written in a sublanguage that is often extremely funny because of the ludicrous errors that result from such inadequate translation practice.

The papers in this present collection all testify to the fact that translation as an activity is always doubly contextualized, since the text has a place in two cultures. Moreover, although idealistically translation may be perceived as a perfect marriage between two different (con)texts, bringing together two entities for better or worse in mutual harmony, in practice translation takes place on a vertical axis rather than a horizontal one. In other words, either the translator regards the task at hand as that of rising to the level of the source text and its author or, as happens so frequently today, particularly where the translator is dealing with texts distanced considerably in time and space, that translator regards the target culture as greater and effectively colonizes the source text. For example, Maria Tymozcko reminds us that cultural appropriation via translation is not confined to the twentieth century, and cites the example of Geoffrey of Monmouth, whilst Mahasweta Sengupta looks at the way in which Rabindranath Tagore shaped his own translations according to the paradigms of imperialist Europe and in so doing lost his own sense of poetry. Piotr Kuhiwczak, in the concluding essay looks at a case study of deliberate ideological shift in translation, where effectively what has taken place is an act of appropriation.

The study of translation practice, therefore, has moved on from a formalist approach and turned instead to the larger issues of context, history and convention. Once upon a time, the questions that were always being asked were 'How can translation be taught?' and 'How can translation be studied?' Those who regarded themselves as translators were often contemptuous of any attempts to teach translation, whilst those who claimed to teach often did not translate and so had to resort to the old evaluative method of setting one translation alongside another and examining both in a formalist vacuum. Now, the questions have changed. The object of study has been redefined; what is studied is the text embedded within its network of both source and target cultural signs and in this way Translation Studies has been able both to utilize the linguistic approach and to move out beyond it. Moreover, with the demise of the notion of equivalence as sameness and recognition of the fact that literary conventions change continuously, the old evaluative norms of 'good' and 'bad', 'faithful' and 'unfaithful' translations are also disappearing. Instead of debating the accuracy of a translation based on linguistic criteria, translators and translation scholars (who hopefully are one and the same) are tending to consider the relative function of the text in each of its two contexts. Ezra Pound realized this a long time ago when he contemptuously dismissed those who criticized him for inaccuracies in his translations, pointing out that if accuracy were the principal criterion of a good translation, then any fool with a bilingual crib could produce just such a result.

Translation/rewriting Studies tend to deal with the constraints that enter into play during the process of both the writing and rewriting of texts. These constraints both belong to the field of literary studies 'proper' and transcend it. They ultimately have to do with power and manipulation, two issues potentially of enormous interest not only to those engaged in literary studies, but also to all their victims outside. The student of translation/rewriting is not engaged in an ever-lengthening and ever more complex dance around the 'always already no longer there'. S/he deals with hard, falsifiable cultural data, and the way they affect people's lives.

Traditionally, the study of translation has been relegated to a small corner within the wider field of that amorphous quasi-discipline known as Comparative Literature. But with the development of Translation Studies as a discipline in its own right, with a methodology that draws on comparatistics and cultural history, the time has come to think again about that marginalization. Translation has been a major shaping force in the development of world culture, and no study of comparative literature can take place without regard to translation. We have both suggested on occasions, with a deliberate intention of subverting the status quo and drawing attention to the importance of Translation Studies, that perhaps we should rethink our notions of Comparative Literature and redefine it as a subcategory of Translation Studies instead of vice versa.

We hope that this collection of essays will provoke further debate about the ways in which literary establishments manipulate originals. Rewriting, as John Frow reminds us is:

[T]he results of a complex articulation of the literary system with other institutions (the school, religion), institutionalized practices (moral or religious training, commemoration, or else a relatively autonomous aesthetic function) and other discursive formations (religious, scientific, ethical). (1986: 182)

Translation is one example of this complex articulation, and an examination of the processes of translation offers a way of understanding how those manipulative shifts take place. Like Proust's grandmother, we all need to feel we can trust a translator; understanding the constraints upon a translator and recognizing the measures that the translator can take in order to escape those constraints is an important step towards establishing that trust. We may not like what we see, but at least we shall not be kept in the dark. At the end of the most violent century in history, when even the air we breathe may be contaminated by forces unknown to us and unseen by us, the more understanding we have of the processes that shape our lives, the more hopeful we can be of a future of greater integrity.

References

Foley, Barbara. (1985) 'The Politics of Deconstruction', in *Rhetoric and Form: Deconstruction at Yale*, ed. Robert Con Davies and Ronald Schleifer. Norman: University of Oklahoma Press.

Foucault, Michel. (1980) *Power/Knowledge*, ed. Colin Gordon. New York: Pantheon Books.

Frow, John. (1986) *Marxism and Literary History*. Cambridge, MA.: Harvard University Press.

Hillis Miller, J. (1987) 'The Triumph of Theory, the Resistance to Reading, and the Question of the Material Base', *PMLA* 102: 281–91.

Johnson, Barbara. (1987) *A World of Difference*. Baltimore and London: Johns Hopkins University Press.

Livingston, P. (1988) *Literary Knowledge*. Ithaca, NY and London: Cornell University Press.

Lyotard, Jean-François. (1985) *The Postmodern Condition*. Minneapolis, MN: University of Minnesota Press.

Merod, Jim. (1987) *The Social Responsibility of the Critic*. Ithaca, NY and London: Cornell University Press.

Proust, Marcel. (1954) *Sodome et Gomorrhe*. Paris: Livre de Poche.

Tompkins, Jane. (1985) *Sensational Designs*. New York: Oxford University Press.

Toury, Gideon. (1980) *In Search of a Theory of Translation*. Tel Aviv: Porter Institute for Poetics and Semiotics.

1. Translation: Its Genealogy in the West

André Lefevere

The history of translation in the West may be said to begin with the production of the Septuagint. Like all early 'historical facts', this one, too, is conveniently shrouded in legend. Conveniently, because the legend will allow us to isolate the basic constraints that have influenced, and continue to influence the history of translation in the West and the other parts of the world it came into contact with.

The Septuagint is the first translation of the Hebrew Old Testament into Greek. It was made by seventy (or seventy-two) translators, all working in separate cells. They all translated the whole text, and all translations turned out to be identical. The translators were sent to Alexandria by Eleazar, High Priest of Jerusalem, at the request of Ptolemy II, Philadelphus, ruler of Egypt. The translation was made for the benefit of those Jewish communities in Egypt who could no longer read the original. It became the basis for later translations into Old Latin, Coptic, Armenian, Georgian and Slavonic.

So far the story. Now for the moral. Translation involves expertise: the seventy translators all produce the same version. They must know their trade. Their knowledge is guaranteed and probably checked by some event beyond their group. A supernatural event most likely, in legend – an all too natural event most likely, in actual fact. Translation also involves commission: a person in authority orders the translation to be made. There are, of course, many instances in which the translator 'auto-commissions' his or her own translation, simply because s/he 'falls' for a text. In this case the problem of 'commission' or at least 'acceptance' of the translation by a publisher is only deferred to the next stage in the process. Translation fills a need: the audience will now be able to read the text again, and the person in authority will have enabled the audience to do so. Translation involves trust: the audience, which does not know the original, trusts that the translation is a fair representation of it. The

audience trusts the experts, and, by implication, those who check on
the experts. As it happened in the case of the Septuagint, this trust
was misplaced. Various versions were found to differ greatly among
themselves, and later versions became so 'Christianized' that the
Jewish communities stopped using the translation altogether. Texts
that start their career as translations do not always remain so, in other
words, but they can remain a central text in the history of a culture.
The King James Bible comes to mind. But the fact that the Septuagint
was, in reality, a 'bad' translation did nothing to undermine its image
– on the contrary, it still is the translation used by the Greek Church
to this day, and it served as the basis for translation into many other
languages of the Ancient Mediterranean world.

The legend of the Septuagint has given us the basic categories of the
history of translation. These categories are: authority (the authority of
the person or institution commissioning or, later, publishing the
translation: the patron; the authority of the text to be translated, in
this case a central text in the source culture; the authority of the writer
of the original, in this case the most absolute authority one can
imagine, and the authority of the culture that receives the translation), expertise, which is guaranteed and checked, trust, which sur-
vives bad translations, and image, the image a translation creates of
an original, its author, its literature, its culture.

Now take the other possibility: a case in which translation is neither
commissioned nor encouraged, but resisted and even forbidden. The
central text in this case is the Koran. No translations of it were allowed
to be made by the faithful. Yet, the original can be said to have had a
pervasive influence on world history, and not just in the area of its
own historical dominance. If the central text is not translated, the
faithful simply have to learn the language of the central text. If they
do not, there will always be experts telling them what is in it,
paraphrasing or interpreting it without actually translating it – but
still creating an image of it. Translations, then, are only one type of
text that makes an 'image' of another text. Other types would be criticism, historiography, commentary and anthologizing. They will be
left out of consideration here. They should not be left out of consideration in studies of translation. The trust readers will have to give to
those experts will have to be greater than the trust they will have to
give to translators, since the possibilities for checking are more
limited.

And then there are the in-between situations. As we know from
history, the Romans translated, but they did not really have to.
Educated Romans could just as well have gone on reading Greek
literature and philosophy in the original, since they were bilingual
anyway. Moreover, the percentage of educated Romans was relatively
small when compared to the total population of the empire, or even

the city of Rome. A similar situation prevailed in the Middle Ages: the learned did not need translation, and they did relatively little of it. In fact, they often did not write in their own language, but translated their thoughts directly into Latin, simply because the conventions of the time demanded this 'reverse translation': one could not be taken seriously as a scholar if one did not write in Latin.

Translation, then, is encouraged and commissioned, resisted and rejected. Obviously the reasons behind these two polar attitudes have little to do with expertise. There must have been Muslims perfectly capable of translating the Koran into other langauges. Trust is a factor, obviously: the central text of a culture should not be tampered with – no graven image should be made of it – precisely because the text guarantees, to a great extent, the very authority of those in authority. Linguistics, therefore, is by no means the overriding consideration in translation history. Translators do not get burnt at the stake because they do not know Greek when translating the Bible. They got burnt at the stake because the way they translated the Bible could be said to be a threat to those in authority.

Before we go on, let us call to mind – and firmly anchor there – the fact that European culture from, say, AD 500 to, say, 1800, was in essence bilingual, or even multilingual. There was a generally respected 'language of authority', first Latin, then French, which would be known by all those professing to be scholars, ecclesiastics or literati. They would know their mother tongues as well, of course, and, in many cases, one or two additional languages. Again, as with the Romans, they would not be all that large in number. European literate culture between 500 and 1800 can therefore be said to have been a bi(multi)lingual coterie culture – a fact so brilliantly repressed by Romantic historians who had to stress the importance of national languages and cultures that it is only now beginning to re-establish itself in the general consciousness of the West.

Obviously, in such a culture, translations were not primarily read for information or the mediation of the foreign text. They were produced and read as exercises, first pedagogical exercises, and, later on, as exercises in cultural appropriation – in the conscious and controlled usurpation of authority. That this usurpation was resented and resisted by those in authority is obvious from remarks like the following, found in the introduction to a translation of Hippocrates' *Aphorisms*: 'even though he foresees that his labour may incur the anger and the mockery of many who seem to be eager to keep the sciences hidden from the people' (Jean Brèche de Tours, in Horguelin, 1981). Members of the coteries who betray the coterie by making its knowledge available to those outside must be prepared to take the consequences of their actions. Jean Brèche de Tours' observation already points forward to the break-up of the coterie culture.

That break-up occurs some time around 1800. After the break-up writers on the subject begin to identify different potential audiences for translations, and different ways of translating emerge to match different audiences. Those who do not know the language of the original, and who are increasingly able to read their own language, will read the translation for information and mediation. Those who still know the language of the original, at least in theory, will read the translation as a short-cut, a crib, or, still, an intellectual and aesthetic challenge, or even game. By 1900, with English increasingly filling the position of 'language of authority' reluctantly given up by French, the trend towards monolingualization of the audience increases, as does the corresponding trend towards producing translations for information. By 1900 the West has also come into contact with languages and cultures for which it has very few experts available. Trust becomes an important factor again, and images can be produced without being subject to rigorous checking. Fitzgerald's appropriation of Omar Khayyam comes to mind.

After 1800, Goethe can write in *Dichtung und Wahrheit:* 'If you want to influence the masses, a simple translation is always best. Critical translations vying with the original really are of use only for conversations the learned conduct among themselves' (in Lefevere, 1977: 38). But the masses do not always want to be influenced. Translations can be, and are still seen as a threat to the identity of a culture, as Victor Hugo observes in his introduction to the Shakespeare translations made by his son, François-Victor:

to translate a foreign poet is to add to one's own poetry; yet this addition does not please those who profit from it. At least not in the beginning; the first reaction is one of revolt. A language into which another idiom is transfused does what it can to resist. (Hugo, 1865: xv)

Not always, though. It does after 1800, and if it feels that the foreign text is a threat to its own authority.

Before 1800, languages were not supposed to resist, nor was translation felt to be an impossible task. On the contrary: Batteux affirms that 'a translator will be forgiven all metamorphoses, on condition that he makes sure that the thought emerges with the same body, the same life' (Batteux, 1824: Vol. II, 242). Language was considered a vehicle for the exchange of thought. Or, in other words, the same thoughts could be conveniently 'dressed' in different languages. The old Latin word for translating: *translatare* can be taken to mean simply: 'an exchange of signifieds' (Berman, 1988: 25), without overmuch regard for the connotations, cultural and otherwise, carried by the actual signifiers. *Translatio*, then, can be seen as epitomizing the ideal of 'faithful translation', so dear to the heart of those in authority, who are intent on purveying the 'right' image of the source text in a different language. *Translatio* is vital for the 'authoritative texts' of a culture:

I insist on treating Holy Writ with such diligence and care because I do not want the oracles of the Holy Ghost to be adulterated by human and earthbound elements. For it is not without divine counsel that they have been expressed in certain selected words, selected from a certain sphere and arranged in a certain order, for there are as many mysteries hidden in them as there are dots in the text. And did not Christ himself say that not one dot should be erased from the Law until heaven and earth are destroyed? (Huetius, 1683: 23)

But *translatio* is impossible. An exchange of signifieds in a kind of intellectual and emotional vacuum, ignoring the cultural, ideological and poetological overtones of the actual signifiers, is doomed to failure, except in texts in which the 'flavour' of the signifiers is not all that important: scholarly texts, or non-literary texts in general. The historical analogy to the Septuagint in this case would be the translational activities of the Spanish school of Toledo, which translated many Arabic scientific and scholarly works into Latin after the city with its magnificent library fell to the Christians. *Translatio* tries to regularize the linguistic components of the translation process, without giving much thought to anything else. If it does, it will shortcircuit as a result of the inbuilt tension between the linguistic and the cultural components of that process.

Its polar opposite can be designated by a Latin word that never really existed: *traductio*. As Berman pointed out: 'Leonardo Bruni is said to have translated the past participle *traductum* used by a Latin author, Aulus Gellius, by the Toscan *tradotto*. But for Aulus Gellius *traductum* did not mean "translated" but rather "transported"' (Berman, 1988: 30). *Traductio* is the more creative counterpart to the more conservative *translatio*. *Traductio* is prepared and allowed to give at least equal weight to the linguistic and the cultural/ideological components of the translation process. It will come to the fore in a culture when that culture considers itself 'authoritative', central with regard to other cultures. But precisely because it usurps that role, that culture will treat the cultural side of the translation process in its *traductio* the way *translatio* treats the linguistic side of the translation process: it will try to regularize it. As Herder puts it in the *Fragmente*:

the French, who are overproud of their natural taste, adapt all things to it, rather than try to adapt themselves to the taste of another time. Homer must enter France a captive, and dress according to fashion, so as not to offend their eyes. He has to allow them to take his venerable beard and his old simple clothes away from him. He has to conform to the French customs, and where his peasant coarseness still shows he is ridiculed as a barbarian. But we, poor Germans, who still are almost an audience without a fatherland, who are still without tyrants in the field of national taste, we want to see him the way he is. (in Lefevere, 1977: 48)

Almost a hundred years later, Fitzgerald writes to his friend E. B. Cowell: 'It is an amusement for me to take what Liberties I like with these Persians who (as I think) are not Poets enough to frighten one from such excursions, and who really do want a little Art to shape them' (Fitzgerald, 1972, VI: xvi). *Traductio* is a matter of the relative weight two cultures carry in the mind of the translator: obviously, Fitzgerald would never have taken the same liberties with a Greek or Roman author, also because there were too many experts around. But since Victorian England considers itself central, and since he happens to be translating from a culture that is by no means central to it, he takes what liberties he pleases. As we shall see later, *traductio* can also be used by translators as individual members of a culture, who are dissatisfied with certain features of it, and want to usurp the authority of texts belonging to another, 'authoritative' culture, to attack those features, defying both experts and those in authority with a certain degree of impunity. In fact, *traductio*, as described by Nicholas Perrot d'Ablancourt in 1709, sounds suspiciously like Eugene A. Nida's 'equivalence of effect': 'I do not always stick to the author's words, nor even to his thoughts. I keep the effect he wanted to reach in mind, and then I arrange matters according to the fashion of our time.' (Perrot d'Ablancourt, 1709: 23).

A view of language, like Schleiermacher's, which no longer sees the signifiers as essentially neutral vehicles for conveying signifieds, but rather as inextricably bound up with different languages, will have to raise the problem of the very possibility of translation. If, as Schleiermacher holds, 'every man is in the power of the language he speaks and all his thinking is a product thereof' (in Lefevere, 1977: 71), translation appears to be an impossible task. Or rather, what appears to be impossible is *translatio*, and all translation will have to be transposition, *traductio*. In his persona of translator, Schleiermacher himself shied away from the consequences of this insight, which makes the second part of his famous maxim, 'move the author towards the reader' the only viable one. But if translation was to remain possible after 1800, it would have to be *traductio*. Possible or not, though, translations continued to be produced, and their production was to keep increasing.

Both *translatio and traductio* involve authority, expertise and trust. Authority draws the ideological parameters of the acceptable. It influences the selection of texts for translating, as well as the ways in which texts are translated. In John of Trevisa's 'Dialogue between a Lord and a Clerk upon Translation' (1903: 23) the Lord makes it quite clear that he is paying the piper, and therefore expects to call the tune. The Lord says: 'I desire not translation of these the best that might be, for that were an idle desire for any man that is now alive, but I would have a skillful translation, that might be known and understood.' In other words, something that works – and, in later words: something that sells. The Clerk just wants to make sure: 'Whether is you liefer have, a translation of these chronicles in rhyme or in prose?' Again, the answer is refreshingly blunt: 'In prose, for commonly prose is more clear than rhyme, more easy and more plain to know and understand.' Translators know who pays the piper, and give advice to other translators accordingly. In a little quoted passage from his best-known work, Du Bellay ends his admonitions to translators with: 'what I say is not meant for those who, at the command of princes and great lords, translate the most famous Greek and Latin writers, since the obedience one owes to those persons admits of no excuse in these matters' (1948: 52). Again about a hundred years later, the Earl of Roscommon refers to those in authority, but they are now of a different kind:

> I pity from my Soul unhappy Men
> Compelled by Want to prostitute their Pen
> Who must, like Lawyers, either starve or plead
> And follow, right or wrong, where Guineas lead.
> (in Steiner, 1975: 82)

Around 1700, with the increasing speed of literacy and the gradual spread of a more open type of society, the authorities are no longer just 'princes and great lords'; they are joined by publishers. If the role of the publisher as the authority who decides what is going to be translated increases, the ideological parameters widen, since the ultimate criterion for deciding is, primarily, money. The publishers of Roscommon's time would publish only a *traductio* of Homer, which would be acceptable/saleable to their readers. Roscommon advises translators to leave out what they deem unacceptable:

> For who, without a Qualm, hath ever lookt
> On Holy Garbage, tho by Homer cookt?
> (in Steiner, 1975: 78)

Similarly, the Abbé Prévost writes in the introduction to his translation of Richardson's *Pamela*:

I have suppressed English customs where they may appear shocking to other nations, or else made them conform to customs prevalent in the rest of Europe. It seemed to me that those remainders of the old and uncouth British ways, which only habit prevents the British themselves from noticing, would dishonor a book in which manners should be noble and virtuous. To give the reader an accurate idea of my work, let me just say, in conclusion, that the seven volumes of the English edition, which would amount to fourteen volumes in my own, have been reduced to four. (in Horguelin, 1981).

It would appear that the French reader will be given a rather different 'image' of Pamela than his English counterpart.

As we move closer to the present, the excesses of *traductio* are more limited. But the case of the translations into English of the Irish national epic, the *Táin*, are a good example of the influence of authority on translation. A scholarly translation of the *Táin* existed in German as early as 1905 (Ernst Windisch's *Die altirische Heldensage 'Táin Bó Cúailnge'*, published in Leipzig). The first comparable translation in English was published only in 1967: Cecile O'Rahilly's *Táin Bó Cúailnge, Recension I*, published in Dublin. The first English *traductio* of the complete *Táin*, by the poet Thomas Kinsella, was published in Dublin in 1969. It had been preceded by many partial *traductiones*, among them Lady Gregory's 1902 version *Cuchulain of Muirthemne*. There were obviously more than enough qualified translators around, but the intellectual and, primarily, emotional climate in Ireland between 1905 and 1969 was such that nobody would translate in its entirety a national epic that alternates descriptions of noble behavior with descriptions of the Irish as a merrily barbaric bunch, killing, looting, raping and defecating all over the place – precisely the image the intellectuals associated with the 'Irish Renaissance' tried to counteract with all their might.

The experts are employed by those in authority to check each other's expertise. This checking process takes place most obviously in the pedagogical situation. As late as the mid-seventeenth century, Gottsched states in his *Ausführliche Redekunst* that translation is 'precisely what the copying of a given model is to a beginner in the art of painting. We know that the works of great masters are copied with pleasure and diligence by mediocre artists or by beginners who would like to make their way' (in Lefevere, 1977: 44). The experts also delimit the poetological parameters of translation: will the finished product be acceptable as literature in the target culture? Will it confirm to the poetics currently dominating that culture? Again, *traductio* appears to be the answer, and some translators go to great lengths to make the source text fit the target culture poetics. De la Motte, for example, states in the introduction to his translation of the *Iliad*:

I have reduced the twenty four books of the *Iliad* to twelve, which are even shorter than Homer's. At first sight you might think that this could only be done at the expense of many important features. But if you pause to reflect that repetitions make up more than one sixth of the *Iliad*, and that the anatomical details of wounds and the long speeches of the fighters make up a lot more, you will be right in thinking that it has been easy for me to shorten the poem without losing any important features of the plot. I flatter myself with the thought that I have done just that, and I even think I have brought together the essential parts of the action in such a way that they are shaped into a whole better proportioned and more sensible in my abbreviated version than in the original. (1714: 17)

Small wonder that Perrot d'Ablancourt, faced with the twin constraints of authority and expertise, began his apology for his translation of Lucian with the diplomatic statement:

Two things can be held against me where this translation is concerned. One has to do with the selection of the work, the other with the way in which I translated it. One group of people will say that I should not have translated this particular author, and another group that I should have translated him differently. (1709: 24)

With the split in the audience after 1800, and the rise of philology as a university discipline, the worst excesses of *traductio* came to an end. The experts could reserve a part of the market for themselves, and produce translations aimed primarily at other experts, in effect recreating the coterie culture, but this time in isolation from the general culture they were part of, even if they would produce the odd *traductio* for its benefit.

The experts are supposed to guarantee that the trust the audience places in various translations is not misplaced. But they are not always successful. The problem is that the audience places less trust in the experts' stamp of approval of a *fida interpretatio* than in the reputation of a translator as a *fidus interpres*. Glyn P. Norton has shown that the well-known Horatian phrase was used earlier by Sallust in the Iugurtha, and that the 'qualifier fidus ... characterizes the personal reliability of the go-between – his mutual trustworthiness in the eyes of both parties – rather than a quality inherent in his translation' (Norton, 1981: 184). This explains why 'bad' translations continue to enjoy great popularity among the general public, even when technically superseded by translations of better quality – a state of affairs which most definitely predates the introduction of copyright. A certain translation achieves a somewhat 'canonized status' and can hardly be dislodged from it. Maybe one of the earliest examples of this state of affairs can be found in St Augustine's seventy-first letter, addressed to Saint Jerome. In the letter, Augustine tells the story of a bishop who introduced the use of Jerome's translation 'in the church of which he is the pastor. They hit upon a passage in the prophet Jonah which you translated very differently from the way in which it has established itself in the mind and memory of all, and the way it had been sung for such a long time.' The result is unrest, foul play is suspected, and after consultation with the local Jews, who are no help either, the bishop 'was forced to correct himself, as if he had made a mistake, since he didn't want to lose all the people in his church' (Augustine, 1909: no. 71).

Translation, then, is sanctioned by authority, but it can also try to subvert authority by usurping the authority of an authoritative text alien to the target culture. The early translations of the *Communist Manifesto* into Russian come to mind, as do the translations of the English philosophers into French in the seventeenth and eighteenth centuries. Translation can play an important part in the struggle betwen rival ideologies, witness Luther's lament in the Tischges-präche:

We are aware of the scribbler in Dresden who stole my New Testament. He admitted that my German is good and sweet and he realized that he could not do better and yet he wanted to discredit it, so he took my New Testament as I wrote it, almost word for word, and he took my preface, my glosses and my name away and wrote his name, his preface and his glosses in their place. He is now selling my New Testament under his name. Oh, dear children, how hurt I was when his prince, in a terrible preface, forbade the reading of Luther's New Testament but ordered the scribbler's New Testament read, which is exactly the same as the one Luther wrote. (in Lefevere, 1977: 22).

Translations also play an important part in the struggle between rival poetics. The case of Pound's *Cathay* (1915) is too well known to warrant extensive discussion here. Faced with Victorian/Edwardian poetics, Pound manufactured the Chinese T'ang dynasty poets as an 'authoritative' countertext, one that did, as if by miracle, fit all the requirements of the new poetry he, Pound, was trying to create. Since translation awards some kind of limited immunity to those who write it (after all, they are not responsible for what others wrote), attacks on the dominant poetics of a literature often pass themselves off as translations. Horace Walpole's *Castle of Otranto (1764)*, the first of the 'Gothic novels', is a case in point. In the preface to the first edition, Walpole tells the reader that the novel he is about to read is a translation of an Italian manuscript, and promises to 'reprint the original Italian' if the novel 'should meet with success' (in Fairclough, 1964: 43). In the preface to the second edition, the author apologizes: 'it is fit that he should ask pardon of his readers for having offered his work to them under the borrowed personage of a translation' (1964: 48). The whole strategem was necessary because of the 'novelty of the attempt ... to blend two kinds of romance, the ancient and the modern' (1964: 48).

Translation usurps authority, but translation also bestows authority. It bestows authority on a language. In Cicero's words:

by giving a Latin form to the text I had read, I could not only make use of the best expressions in common usage with us, but I could also coin new expressions, analogous to those used in Greek, and they were no less well received by our people, as long as they seemed appropriate. (Cicero, *De Oratore*, book I: 35)

Translation forces a language to expand, and that expansion may be welcome as long as it is checked by the linguistic community at large. Translation can also bestow the authority inherent in a 'language of authority' (Latin, French, English/Russian) on a text originally written in another language, which lacks that authority. Many works written in 'minor' languages, such as Strindberg's dramas, would not belong to 'world literature' if they had not been launched in a language of authority, in this case French. Similarly, Ibsen's dramas were introduced to Europe not in his native Norwegian, but in German by the Volksbühne in Berlin. The pervasive influence of translation is so great that these works cease, after a while, to be thought of as 'foreign' to the 'language of authority'. English departments now routinely teach both Ibsen and Strindberg, and students tend to find the Scandinavian names a bit of a nuisance, at times. As a cumulative effort, translation eventually builds up a translinguistic and transcultural canon (the 'Penguin Classics' in our day and age) which is, in its turn, invested with authority.

Translation also allows writers in the target culture to 'proceed on the authority' of writers alien to the target culture and introduced into it by translators. In other words, translation introduces new devices in the literatures by which it is received. The sonnet, for example, was introduced into Chinese in the 1920s, via Feng Chi's translations. The ode became the major genre of the poets of the *Pléiade* after it had been translated extensively from Greek and Latin. Translation, under the moralizing aegis of the Jesuits, transformed the picaresque novel into the *Bildungsroman* in Germany. The alternation of masculine and feminine rhymes in French goes back to Octavien de St Gelais' translations of Ovid. The hexameter was introduced into German by the Homer translations of Johann Heinrich Voss. John Hookham Frere's translations of Pulci reintroduced *ottava rima* into English, where it was soon to be used by Byron in his *Don Juan*. Yet Goethe's pious 'hope that literary history will plainly state who was the first to take this road in spite of so many obstacles' (in Lefevere, 1977: 39), tends to remain exactly that. Literary histories, as they have been written until recently, have had little time for translations, since for the literary historian translation has had to do with 'language' only, not with literature – another pernicious outgrowth of the 'monolingualization' of literary history by Romantic historiographers intent on creating 'national' literatures preferably as uncontaminated as possible by foreign influences. Yet on every level of the translation process it can be shown that if linguistic considerations conflict with considerations of an ideological and/or poetiological nature, the latter considerations tend to win. A. W. Schlegel's fateful pronouncement that 'one of the first principles of the art of translation is that, for as far as the nature of a language allows, a poem should be recreated in the same meter' (in Lefevere, 1977: 52), which has been responsible for all kinds of metrical contortions in translations made roughly between 1830 and 1930, was obviously not made on linguistic grounds. Browning's insistence on the 'use of certain allowable constructions which, happening to be out of daily favour, are all the more appropriate to archaic workmanship (Browning, 1937: 1095) is responsible for the fact that most Victorian translations of the classics read so monotonously alike. It was not inspired by linguistic necessity, but by the desire to acquire the timeless through use of the archaic. The result did not meet with the translators' expectations.

The creation of the Latin word *sacramentum* is also revealing in this respect. When the early Christians needed to translate the Greek word *musterion*, they did not want simply to Latinize it, because it was too close to the vocabulary used by the 'mystery cults' which were Christianity's main competition at the time. For the same reason they rejected words like *sacra, arcana, initia*, which would have been semantically acceptable equivalents. They hit on *sacramentum* as a term both neutral and close to the original. But when St Jerome prepared the Vulgate, Christianity had won the battle against the mystery religions, and he felt free to simply Latinize *musterion*. (cf. Klopsch, 1983: 37–8) Similarly, the Aramaic Jesus Christ is supposed to have spoken did not have a copula. He can therefore never have said: 'This is my body' when pointing at a loaf of bread. The copula was put in by translators for both linguistic and ideological reasons.

That different types of text need to be translated in different stylistic (not linguistic) ways, was recognized by Gaspard de Tende as early as 1660. 'It would not be advisable,' he says, 'to translate orations that need to be treated with some leeway into a precise style, cut and dry, nor should you translate parables, that need to be short and precise, into a style that would allow them more leeway' (de Tende, 1665: 5).

Finally, untranslatability seems to have a lot more to do with the absence of poetologial equivalents than with the absence of semantic or morphosyntactic equivalents. The *qasida*, the canonized genre of Arabic poetry, has never been satisfactorily translated in the West, because it has no obvious generic equivalent. This is how Ibn Qutaiba, the Arab poet and critic, describes the genre:

the composer . . . began by mentioning the deserted dwelling places and the relics and traces of habitation. Then he wept and complained and addressed the desolate encampment and begged his companions to make a halt, in order that he might have occasion to speak of those who had once lived there and afterwards departed. . . . Then to this he linked the erotic prelude and bewailed the violence of his love and the anguish of separation from his mistress and the extremity of his passion and desire, so as to win the hearts of his hearers and divert their eyes towards him and invite their hearts to listen to him. . . . He followed up his advantage and set forth his claim: thus he went on to complain of fatigue and want of sleep and travelling by night and of the noonday heat, and how his camel had been reduced to leanness. And after representing all the discomfort and danger of his journey, he knew that he had finally justified his hope and expectation of receiving his due meed from the person to whom the poem was addressed, he entered upon the panegyric and incited him to reward, and kindled his generosity by exalting him above his peers and pronouncing the greatest dignity, in comparison with his, to be little. (in Arberry, 1957: 15–16)

It is easy to discover both ideological and poetological elements in this description that would be most unfamiliar to the Western reader. Lyall states that the *qasida* 'is not epic, nor even narrative . . . still less is it dramatic . . . the Greek idyll is perhaps the type which comes nearest to it in classical poetry' (1930: xviii). Nicholson calls it an 'ode' (1922: 76) and Jones refers to 'casseidas or eclogues' (1807: X: 341).

Language is not the problem. Ideology and poetics are, as are cultural elements that are not immediately clear, or seen as completely 'misplaced' in what would be the target culture version of the text to be translated. One such element is the camel dung mentioned in Labid's *qasida*, which can hardly be expected to make a 'poetic' impression on Western readers. Carlyle, the English Victorian translator, leaves it out altogether; to him 'this was simply incomprehensible' (Polk, 1974: xxviii). German translators, on the other hand, try to find a cultural analogy, but with little success: the solution is worse than the problem: 'German scholars, familiar with the peasants of their own land, where the size of the dung heap is some indication of the prosperity of the farmer, merely transported to the desert the social values of Bavaria' (Polk, 1974: xxviii). Most attempts at surveying translation history begin with a pious platitude. This attempted survey ends with one, borrowed from Mme de Staël: 'the most eminent service one can render to a literature, is to transport the masterpieces of the human spirit from one language to another' (de Staël: 328) Pious platitudes invariably surface in discussions of translation, not just because the subject is so complex, but also because it is potentially disturbing: it keeps questioning expertise and it is always potentially subversive of authority. This does not make it exactly a popular topic for research, but it does make it a potentially very rewarding one.

Translation is one of the most obvious forms of image making, of manipulation, that we have. It makes its images together with other media. For many people in the English-speaking world, for example, *Crime and Punishment* will always be an amalgam of some of the following: the Constance Garnett or the Magarshack translation, histories of Russian literature, articles in mass circulation magazines, television classical drama series. Translation is responsible to a large extent for the image of a work, a writer, a culture. Together with historiography, anthologizing and criticism it prepares works for inclusion in the canon of world literature. It introduces innovations into a literature. It is the main medium through which one literature influences another. It can be potentially subversive and it can be potentially conservative. It can tell us about the self-image of a culture at a given time, and the changes that self-image undergoes. It can tell us about the strength of a poetics and/or an ideology at a certain time, simply by showing us the extent to which they were interiorized by people writing translations at that time (poor vilified De la Motte was not trying to demolish Homer; he was simply trying to be a 'good' writer as best he knew how). Translation can tell us a lot about the power of images and the ways in which images are made, about the ways in which authority manipulates images and employs experts to sanction that manipulation and to justify the trust of an audience – which is why the study of translation can teach us a few things not just about the world of literature, but also about the world we live in.

References

Arberry, Arthur J. (1957) *The Seven Odes*. London and New York: Allen and Unwin and Macmillan.

Augustine, (1909) 'Letter to Jerome', in *The Letters of St Augustine*, ed. W. J. Sparrow-Simpson. London: Society for Promoting Christian Knowledge.

Batteux, Charles (1824) *Principes de littérature*, 5 vols. Paris.

Berman, Antoine (1988) 'De la translation à la traduction', *Etudes sur le texte et ses transformations* 1: 23–40.

Browning, Robert (1937) 'The Agamemnon of Aeschylus' (1877), *The Poetical Works of Robert Browning*. New York: Macmillan.

De la Motte, Houdar (1714) *L'Iliade*. Amsterdam.

De Tende, Gaspard (1665) *Règles de la traduction*. Paris.

Du Bellay, Joachim (1948) *Défense et illustration de la langue française*. Paris: Didier.

Fairclough, William (ed.) (1964) *Three Gothic Novels*. Harmondsworth: Penguin Books.

Fitzgerald, Edward (1972) *The Variorum and Definitive Edition of the Poetical and Prose Writings*, 7 vols. New York: Doubleday.

Horguelin, Antoine (ed.) (1981) *Anthologie de la manière de traduire*. Montreal: Linguatech.

Huetius, Petrus Danielus (1683) *De optimo genere interpretandi libri duo*. The Hague.

Hugo, Victor (1865) 'Préface de la nouvelle traduction de Shakespeare', in *Oeuvres complètes de William Shakespeare*, trans. François Victor Hugo, 15 vols. Paris: Pagnerre.

Jones, William (1980) *The Works of Sir William Jones*. London, 1807, 13 vols; repr. Delhi: Agam Prakashan Reprint.

Klopsch, Paul (1983) 'Die mitellateinische Lyrik', in *Lyrik des Mittelalters*, ed. Heinz Bergner, 2 vols. Stuttgart: Reclam.

Lefevere, André (ed. and trans.) (1977) *Translating Literature: The German Tradition*. Assen: Van Gorcum.

Lyall, Charles J. (ed. and trans.) (1930) *Translations of Ancient Arabian Poetry*. New York: Columbia University Press.

Nicholson, Reynold A. (ed. and trans.) (1922) *Translations of Eastern Poetry and Prose*. Cambridge: Cambridge University Press.

Norton, Glynn P. (1981) 'Humanist Foundations of Translation Theory', *Canadian Review of Comparative Literature* 8: 173–91.

Perrot d'Ablancourt, Nicholas (1709) *Lucien. De la traduction*. Amsterdam.

Polk, William R. (ed. and trans.) (1974) *The Golden Ode by Labid Ibn Rabiah*. Chicago: University of Chicago Press.

de Staël, Mme. (1821) *Mélange*, Oeuvres complètes, Paris.

Steiner, T. R. (ed.) (1975) *English Translation Theory 1650–1800*. Assen: Van Gorcum.

Trevisa, John of (1903) 'Dialogue between a Lord and a Clerk upon Translation', in *Fifteenth Century Prose and Verse*, ed. A. W. Pollard. Westminster: Constable.

2 Translation: Text and Pre-Text 'Adequacy' and 'Acceptability' in Crosscultural Communication

Palma Zlateva

Let me note, at the outset, that the terms 'adequacy' and 'acceptability' as used in this paper do not allow for a statement like the following: 'A translated text can be located on an axis between the two hypothetical poles of adequacy (source text oriented) or acceptability (target language oriented)' (Toury, 1980: 34). Such a statement seems to exclude the possibility that a translated text could ever be both adequate to the original and acceptable in the target language, since a +adequate translation will always be a −acceptable one. This logically leads to the conclusion that the only translated text to satisfy the conditions for being a metatext will be a translated text situated right in the middle of this axis, where we can only have zero adequacy and zero acceptability.

I shall try to supply arguments in favour of another option, namely that the acceptability of a translated text in the target language should be considered part of the adequacy of its translation. *Any adequately translated literary text becomes a material fact not only in the target language, but in the target literature as well: it exists in both. The fact of its existence and acceptability in the target language, however, does not necessarily imply that it is, or will be, immediately accepted in the target literature and culture.* This is a different matter altogether. It has to do with the translator's choice of a particular work at a particular time, with the core and periphery of the target cultural and literary tradition at that particular moment, and with several other factors. In short, it pertains to considerations located both on the level of pre-text and post-text.

Peter Pan, that favourite of several generations of English children, failed to attract the interest and win the admiration of its Bulgarian readers. Its heroes did not become part of their universe of discourse in the way Winnie the Pooh did. The reason for this has nothing to do with the quality of the *Peter Pan* translation. Rather, Winnie the Pooh and his friends are just animal toys that exist in any child's world, without being exclusively English. In Bulgarian the little teddy bear is called Mecho Puh, which is probably better than the transliteration Vini Puh, under which it is familiar to children in Russia. Yet, translated or transliterated, it is just a name, and children can and do choose the strangest of names for their toys and pets. Winnie was created and came to life in English literature and entered English culture only via literature. Peter Pan, on the other hand, is not just a literary hero, but a myth, which he had been long before J. M. Barrie wrote down his stories. He was an image, 'interweaving lots of threads, old and new': literature, folklore, fairy-tale allusions and motifs as well as children's games and superstitions:

They all figure in *Peter Pan*, providing its particular aroma of recognition, so very important for the child's imagination. By introducing all these themes as long familiar, generally accepted and almost as real as everyday life, Barrie gives his story an impetus, encouraging children to build countless fantasies on this firm and familiar basis. (Demurova, 1986: 12)

It is precisely this 'firm and familiar' basis that is lacking for Bulgarian children who try to understand *Peter Pan* and to appreciate Barrie's talent as a storyteller. We cannot blame the translators for failing to elicit an effect in their readers similar to the effect the original made on its readers, since this effect is the result of something very much not part of the actual text the translators had to deal with. Their translation failed to be integrated into the receiving culture, but the verdict 'unacceptable' has nothing to do with the quality of the translation as such. On the other hand, many somewhat less than adequate translations have, for one reason or another, become perfectly acceptable texts in the target culture, which they provide with a somewhat skewed version of the original.

The fate of Alejo Carpentier's story 'Viaje a la semilla' is also significant in this line of argument. When it was translated for the first time, ten years ago, Bulgarian publishers liked the story and its translation, but decided it had to be rearranged so as to start with 'la semilla' and then proceed to the moment of the actual storytelling. The 'consensus', therefore, which was authorized to evaluate the perfectly adequate translation, took the liberty of changing the structure of the original story, rendering it acceptable to the then dominant literary tradition, or poetics – or rather, to what it regarded as such, and tried to impose.

The part played by this type of 'consensus' in judging the acceptability of (translated) literary texts can hardly be overestimated,
especially in a society with a highly centralized publishing industry.
In Bulgaria the name and writings of Franz Kafka were familiar only
to a limited group of specialists, long after the works of his (mainly
South American) epigones had been translated into Bulgarian,
accepted with enthusiasm and imitated in their turn by Bulgarian
writers. When, finally, literary and aesthetic considerations prevailed
over considerations of a more ideological nature and Kafka's own
writings were actually made available in translation, they were met by
the broader reading public with a fair degree of indifference.

The pre-text and post-text problems touched upon, as well as the
problems which arise during the production of the actual text of the
translation, result from the profound difference in communicative
situation between an author and the reader of his prototext on the one
hand, and an author and the reader of the translation, or metatext, on
the other. An author constructs a world based on the inventory of her
native language and for an audience which shares her universe of
discourse. The reader is presented with a text in her native language,
which she is able to decode and judge in terms both of language and
universe of discourse, no matter whether the author on occasion
violates either, or both.

When a translator plays the part of the reader, on the other hand,
she must apply both her knowledge and her intuition to the author's
universe of discourse, very conscientiously, but also very cautiously.
The translator's knowledge is very often not the result of direct
observation, but rather the result of information about the author's
universe of discourse acquired from other texts. In practice the
translator often knows more about the literary tradition the author
writes in, but less about his living reality. A brilliant (and hilarious)
illustration of this fact can be found in the numerous letters Akira
Sazaki, the translator, sends to Ronald Frobisher, the author, in
David Lodge's *Small World*.

Only when you translate, or edit translations, do you realize how
indispensable the translator's experience of the author's world is. The
British, for instance, unlike the rest of the world, drive on the left. But
it takes time to master the habit of looking right instead of left when in
Britain. One more consequence of this state of affairs is that it is
equally strange for the British to look left first, a habit fully interiorized by the rest of the world – except for South Africa. Sometimes this
very difference is thematized in a fictional text:

The glory of his adventure needs, after all, a reflector, someone capable of
registering the transformation of the dim Rummidge lecturer into Visiting
Professor Philip Swallow, member of the academic jet-set, ready to carry

English culture to the far side of the globe at the drop of an airline ticket. And for once he will have the advantage of Boon, in his previous experience of America. Boon will be eager for advice and information: *about looking left first when crossing the road, about 'public school' meaning the opposite of what it means in England, and 'knock up' meaning something entirely different.* (Lodge, 1986: 37)

Though simple on the linguistic level, this passage will present serious problems to the translator trying to translate it for a non-British audience. She will hardly be able to translate it 'well' if she is not at least as familiar with the author's universe of discourse as with his tradition, language and literature. In other words, the communication between the translator as a reader of the prototext and the author, although still within the boundaries of the intralingual, is already a crosscultural communication. For the translator, even if she has mastered the author's language and tradition in detail and knows everything about his world, is still the carrier of another language and another tradition, living in another world. She can therefore perform the functions of a mediator in the interlinguistic and crosscultural communication between an author and his readers in another culture which uses another language. The primary communication between the author and his translator, and the secondary metacommunication between the translator as an author of the translated text and her reader, are the two main stages in this complex process. The process consists of many other sub-stages, and I shall try to illustrate by means of example that failure in each of these results in deviations on the level of adequacy.

It should be noted that the source language and the target language usually have some common features, as do the author's and the translator's universes of discourse. These common features overlap in different ways, depending on both the language pairs in question, and a number of historical, ethnical and sociopolitical factors. Besides, the author constructs his universe of discourse in his very own way; the translator has to take his style and his outlook into account, and analyse the individual characteristics of a particular text as compared to those of the author's other writings. Consequently: 'the literary translator has to know literature, just as the translator of biochemical texts has to know biochemistry' (Lefevere, 1982: 5).

Sherwood Anderson's Bulgarian translator obviously lacked such knowledge, although her translation of *Winesburg, Ohio* was favourably received by the consensus of Bulgarian critics. Knowing that Anderson is regarded as a classic, she introduced into her translation different archaic words and structures, many synonymous verbs and adjectives so colourful and outdated that they represent an obstacle to any smooth reception of the Bulgarian text. As a result the style of her translation has become so authorial that it differs drastically from the unadorned, conscientiously simplified and concise style of the American author. Let me quote only the second and third paragraphs of the original:

Quite a fuss was made about the matter. The carpenter, who had been a soldier in the Civil War, came into the writer's room and sat down *to talk of* building a platform for the purpose of *raising the bed*. The writer had cigars lying about and the carpenter smoked. For a time the two men *talked* of the *raising of the bed* and then they *talked* of other things. The soldier got on the *subject of the war*. The writer, in fact, led him to *that subject*. The carpenter had once been a prisoner in Andersonville prison and had lost a brother. The brother had died of starvation, and whenever the carpenter got upon *that subject* he *cried*. He, like the old writer, had a white mustache, and when he *cried* he puckered up his lips and the mustache bobbed up and down.

Koleckova's 1985 translation reads:

Mnogo se suetiha okolo taya rabota. Durvodeletsat, edno vreme voinik viv Grazhdanskata voina, vleze pri pistaleyia i sedna *da pogovoryat* za napravata na postavka, *vruz koyato da kachat legloto*. Pisatelyat imashe puri v stayata i durvodeletsat sapushi. Dvamata *poumuvaha* izvestno vreme *kak da natukmyat legloto*, a posle *zabubriha* za drugi neshta. Nyakogashniyat voinik *podhvana prikazka za voinata*. Vsushtnost pisatelyat go navede na *tazi tema*. Edno vreme durvodeletsat lezhal v zatvora na Andersunvil i zagubil brat si. Brat mu se pominal ot glad i kogato i da zagovoreshe *za nego*, durvodeletsat *se razplakvashe*. I toi kato stariya pisatel imashe beli mustatsi i kato *ridaeshe*, hapeshe ustni i mustatsite mu podskachaha nagore-nadolu.

There is nothing archaic or ornamental in the English text. Each of the italicized words has been used at least twice, presumably to achieve a certain effect. Yet in the translation the repetition that is a characteristic feature of the original is avoided as much as possible. 'To talk' is rendered by 'da pogovoryat', by 'poumuvaha' (to speculate), and by 'zabubriha' (to chatter). 'To raise the bed' becomes 'da kachat legloto', but also 'da natukmyat legloto' (to fix up, adjust). 'The subject of the war' and 'that subject' are turned into 'prikazka za voinata', 'tazi tema', and 'za nego' (about him, i.e. the dead brother). 'To cry' is translated as 'razplakvashe' (began crying) and 'ridaeshe' (to wail). The Bulgarian verbs do not just name the action, but describe it in one way or another as taking place in a certain manner. Besides, in Bulgarian, women usually 'bubrya' or 'ridaya', not men.

If the Bulgarian reader of this translation were to be told that Hemingway, Faulkner, Wolfe, Steinbeck and Caldwell are all followers of a tradition established in American fiction by Sherwood Anderson, she will simply not believe it. The chain 'author–translator–receiver' has already been interrupted on the level of analysis. As a result the translation strategy chosen on the second level – that of synthesizing the new text by means of the target language – has proved inadequate. Consequently, this kind of translation is not functionally equivalent to the original, and the relation between the two is not that of metatext to prototext. Yet this text was accepted into Bulgarian literature, in which a style of writing known as 'Hemingway's' had been accepted, appreciated and imitated long before the present (mis)representation of his predecessor was published. This deprives the translator's 'infidelity' of the possible excuse that she has abandoned adequacy for the sake of acceptability.

One of the reasons why translations of this kind are not only accepted but often praised for the 'beauty and richness of their language' – the standard line in any review which bothers with the quality of the translation – is the fact that very few of the literary critics know the language in which the book they are discussing has been written. Consequently, they are not in a position to judge the translation as such, but only as a text in their native language. In other words, instead of being even greater experts than the translator in both their own language and culture as well as those of the original, they find themselves in the position of the ordinary reader for whom the translated text is a source of information not just about the author's world and his outlook, but also about his language.

It follows that the criteria for judging adequacy of language use in translation are much more complex than those by which we evaluate the use of language in an original work of literature. The language of a translation is good when, and only when, the translator has managed adequately to render the original's overall content, both aesthetic and conceptual. Only then is the translation a maximally close analogue of the original text.[1]

If we accept adequate translation and mistranslation as the two poles of a hypothetical scale of adequacy, we can situate translations with different degrees of adequacy in between. These translations will be seen to deviate to a different degree from the different norms set up by the original or established in the target language and culture. As has been shown, deviations from the first type of norms – those set up by the original – may remain unnoticed by readers, and even by critics. Deviations from the second type of norms – those of the target language and culture – may be required by a given element in the text of the original, and are then perfectly acceptable in the translation. Witness the following example, taken from the film version of A. J. Cronin's *The Captain's Doll*. The captain's wife has identified his mistress and exclaims in triumph: 'As soon as I saw the doll, the cat was out of the bag!' This was subtitled in Bulgarian as: 'Shtom vidyah kuklata, *kotkata izskochi ot torbata*!'

The Bulgarian audience tried in vain to spot either *kotka* (a cat) or *torba* (a bag) on the screen. They were not supposed to know that 'a cat in a bag' is a metaphorical expression for something kept in the dark. But the translator should have known and he should have tried to substitute an analogous idiom in Bulgarian. Or he should have rendered at least the meaning, even at the expense of the stylistic colouring if such an idiom proved to be non-existent.

This was an example of mistranslation, the pole beyond which we cannot speak of translation as such. The translator has failed to decode the source text correctly, because he did not know the source language well enough. As a result, the translation is unacceptable, but not because its wording violates any norms of Bulgarian language or culture. It is unacceptable because it is not a reflection (however distorted) of the original. Not knowing the universe of discourse of an author and his heroes can be just as dangerous a source of mistranslation as not knowing his language. After Watergate, for instance, the word 'plumber' developed the meanings of 'spy, secret agent', and for utterly non-linguistic reasons. The men who planted the bugging devices were disguised as plumbers. Since he did not know this, the translator of another movie rendered the word by its dictionary equivalent, *vodoprovodchik*, which did not correspond in any way to anything taking place on the screen.

It is absurd to expect, of course, that a translator can be very familiar with all the specific spheres of life an author may choose to explore. Few, if any, Bulgarian specialists in the English language and culture can claim to know as much as Arthur Haley does about the management of hotels, hospitals or airports. But they know enough to find out just what they do not know and cannot cope with, and to consult specialists in the coresponding areas. As a result, Bulgarians are now reading quite adequate, readable and, therefore, bestselling translations of *Airport*, *The Final Diagnosis* and *Hotel*.

Hemingway's *The Old Man and the Sea* has been less fortunate. Not only did it not occur to its translators to consult an ichthyologian, they do not seem to have properly consulted their English dictionaries. As a result, the names of the fish the old man catches or fails to catch are a source of utter confusion to them. This is not just a matter of mistranslation or 'loss', since 'loss occurs in all forms of communication, whether it involves translation or not' (Lefevere, 1982: 11). Perhaps the worst mistake is made in connection with the dolphin. Hemingway describes expertly – even lovingly – the way in which the old man catches, kills and eats it, but his Bulgarian translators call the dolphin *delfin* throughout. True enough, the first dictionary equivalent listed for 'dolphin' is 'porpoise-like sea mammal', arguably the most friendly and intelligent of sea creatures, but this 'dolphin' does not look at all like the fish described in the text. The translators needed the word *dorado* instead, which fits both the first *and* second equivalents listed in the dictionary: 'a fish noted for its changes in colour in dying'. The old man even calls the fish *dorado* himself. The translators interpret the Spanish word as an epithet and explain in a footnote that it means 'golden'. There is no denying that the name *dorado* sounds exotic in Bulgarian and is known only to a limited group of specialists, since there are no 'doradoes' in the Black Sea – yet the discrepancy is so glaring that the translators should have been alerted to it. As it happens, they are to blame for something far more damaging than just the wrong word: they are to blame for the wrong image.

In conclusion, let me discuss some deviations from the norms of the target language which are not called for by the original text and which are not the result of any failure on the translator's part to decode its message. In other words, I shall be pointing out instances of 'noise' in the communication channel. Such deviations are sometimes classified in three groups: (1) the utterance is acceptable, but in a different situation; (2) the utterance is acceptable, but is not normally uttered by this person; (3) the utterance is acceptable, but nobody would make it.

When introduced to her lover's wife, the heroine of *The Captain's Doll* utters the usual 'how do you do' *after* she has given her name, as is usual in English. The translator subtitled: 'Johana Tsurasenlou. Zdraveite.' The normal Bulgarian phrase would first express pleasure at meeting the person; only then would the speaker give her name.

'Oh stop playing the gentleman, Bob' has been translated as 'Ah, nedei se durzha tolkova kavalerski s men, Bob!' Several objections could be made to the translation. The speaker is downright rude to his interlocutor and he is a gentleman not *s* (with, towards) but *pred* (him) i.e. in his presence or, literally: 'in front of him'. The exclamation 'Ah' is normally used only by women or gays. The whole phrase sounds very clumsy indeed in Bulgarian.

In closing, let me briefly recapitulate:

I have pointed out some of the specific features of translation as a peculiar type of interlingual communication, involving representatives of two linguistically different cultures.

I have discussed the difference between the original reader of the prototext and the translator, whose knowledge of the author's universe of discourse is often primarily theoretical.

I have accepted the basic notions of 'adequacy' and 'acceptability', but I have tried to prove that they are not polar opposites.

Instead of an axis with 'adequacy' and 'acceptability' as its poles, I suggest another axis, or rather, a cline with 'adequacy' as one pole and 'mistranslation' as the other.

Between those two poles translations are produced with different degrees of adequacy. For various reasons these translations deviate in one way or another from the norms set up by the original or established in the target language.

Some of the 'noise' in the communication channel results from the lack of what we take for granted in our native tongue: knowledge of the norms of its substrata, in all its spheres of application and in different situations involving different people.

Notes

1. On the notion of 'analogue' in translation, see Anna Lilova (1981) *Uvod v obshtata teoriya na prevoda*. Sofia.

References

Demurova, N. (1986) 'Ja yunost, ja radost . . .' (*Peter Pan*). Moscow: Raduga Publishers.

Lefevere, André, (1982) 'Translated Literature', *Dispositio* 19–20–21: 3–22.

Lodge, David. (1986) *Changing Places*. Harmondsworth: Penguin Books.

Toury, Gideon. (1980) *In Search of a Theory of Translation*. Tel Aviv: Porter Institute for Poetics and Semiotics.

3 Translation and the Consequences of Scepticism

Anne Mette Hjort

Valid theories of translation should entail certain consequences for the actual practice of translation. Such implications are, however, difficult to articulate in positive terms when the arguments in question derive their force from one of the various brands of philosophical scepticism. In what follows, I shall focus uniquely on Quine's discussion of radical translation problems as they bear on a more general philosophy of language and translation. I do, however, assume that Quine's sceptical arguments are in some sense paradigmatic and that my claims concerning their logical consequences remain pertinent to other cases. Essentially, my argument comprises three broad moves. First I establish a standard account of Quine's position on radical translation. Next I develop two different ways of interpreting the consequences of Quine's sceptical argument. I argue that only one of these two interpretations draws on a correct understanding of the nature of sceptical arguments. Finally, I try to show that if we construe the consequences of scepticism in terms of what I shall call a 'moderate fallibilism' then sceptical arguments prove wholly compatible with a pragmatic turn. Indeed, sceptical arguments may be usefully mobilized in order to bring the pragmatic (i.e. the political and institutional) dimensions of translation to the fore.

Let us, then, begin by trying to grasp how Quine's argument concerning radical translation problems is supposed to work. Quine's position is typically understood to turn on two related theses:

(1) Theory is underdetermined by all possible evidence. That is, mutually exclusive physical theories may account equally well for the available evidence. In the case of translation, this means that 'manuals for translating one language into another can be set up in divergent ways, all compatible with the totality of speech dispositions, yet incompatible with one another' (Quine, 1960: 27).

(2) The referents of terms are inscrutable. Here the claim is that semantic synonymy cannot be inferred from stimulus synonymy. It is sometimes assumed that this proposition holds only with respect to those contexts of translation in which the problems are *radical* in nature. According to this line of reasoning, the inscrutability of reference thesis would pertain primarily to cases such as the following: an anthropologist observing the speech behaviour of two individuals belonging to an alien culture would be unwarranted in concluding that *gavagai* means 'rabbit' just because both agents respond to the same stimulus – the presence of a rabbit and the pointing gesture of the anthropologist – with an utterance of the term *gavagai*. According to the sceptic, the anthropologist has no way of knowing whether *gavagai* refers to the whole rabbit, to rabbitdom, to undetached rabbit parts, and so on. Nor does he have any basis for assuming that the referent intended by one of the speakers corresponds exactly to those envisaged by other speakers within the foreign community being observed. This, I take it, is essentially the point of the claim that 'two men could be just alike in all their dispositions to verbal behavior under all possible sensory stimulations, and yet the meanings or ideas expressed in their identically sounded utterances could diverge radically, for the two men, in a wide range of cases' (Quine, 1960: 26). It is clear, then, from Quine's statements in *Word and Object* and elsewhere that the inscrutability of reference thesis should not be limited to problems of radical translation alone and is, in fact, more general in its scope. For example, Quine insists that semantic synonymy cannot be inferred from dispositional synonymy even in those cases where the speakers are bilinguals having the same languages in common (1960: 74).[1]

As I see it, the sceptical problem articulated by Quine has the issue of justification at its core and proceeds by means of a twofold strategy. On the one hand, it establishes strict criteria for valid justifications. On the other, it claims that all philosophical attempts to meet these criteria involve metaphysical or ontological presuppositions that themselves are without foundation. It is in this respect that Quine's argument may be said to be anti-foundationalist. All possible justifications can themselves be made the subject of the sceptic's doubts. As we know, the claim is *not* that we do not translate nor that we should not translate. Indeed, Quine points to the existence of certain 'regulative maxims' and 'analytic hypotheses' that help us determine how we should proceed when confronted by foreign terms that must be appropriately rendered in a given target language. Dictionaries, manuals and grammars all contain transformational rules that establish the social appropriateness of some translations and the unacceptability of others. The point of the sceptical argument is not to prove that the conditions of a given activity cannot be satisfied, but to show that the practice in question cannot be given an ultimate justification or grounding.

Now, what are the implications of Quine's sceptical argument for the practice of translation? In sketching an answer to this question, we may usefully refer to Saul Kripke's distinction between 'straight' and 'sceptical' solutions to sceptical problems. Following Kripke, we may call a 'proposed solution to a sceptical philosophical problem a *straight* solution if it shows that on closer examination the scepticism proves to be unwarranted; an elusive or complex argument proves the thesis the sceptic doubted' (Kripke, 1982: 66). A sceptical solution, on the other hand, 'begins ... by conceding that the sceptic's assertions are unanswerable' (1982: 66). The sceptical solution hinges on showing that the practice in question does not require the type of justification demanded by the sceptic.

In what follows I shall explore a sceptical solution to the problem of translation as posed by Quine. This does not, of course, mean that straight solutions may be ruled out in advance.[2] They do, however, represent a tall order indeed, in so far as they would appear to involve proving the true nature of the following kinds of thesis:

1. When speakers utter words in a language that we speak and understand, we always know with complete certainty exactly what they mean.
2. When one term is substituted for another we can always prove that no other term could possibly have conveyed the intended meaning at least as well, if not better.

The list could be endlessly expanded. My point is that the sceptic's argument cannot be readily answered by means of a negation of any one of its central propositions. It remains, then, for us to ask whether a sceptical solution can be provided for Quine's sceptical problem. I shall return to this issue when I discuss the moderate fallibilism which, in my mind, follows from Quine's doctrine. First, however, it is useful to explore an alternate conception of the consequences of Quine's scepticism. Understanding exactly what is missed by this imprudent scepticism will allow us to see more clearly what is gained by a moderate fallibilism.

What, then, is 'imprudent scepticism' and how does it relate to Quine's philosophical problem? We may begin to address ourselves to this issue by looking at a sceptical question which, although outlandish, figures frequently in the philosophical debates: 'how can you prove or how can you know, with apodictic certainty, that you are not a brain in a vat?' Now, imprudent scepticism is what results from a response that involves the following two moves: (1) I cannot prove with apodictic certainty that I am not a brain in a vat and (2) therefore I am a brain in a vat. Now, many of us, I believe, feel that some version of (1) constitutes an appropriate or legitimate response to the question. Proposition (2), however, seems wholly unsound. The error consists of eliminating the interrogative dimension of the sceptical challenge so as to articulate a substantive empirical thesis in its stead.

Although the logical flaw involved in affirming (2) lies at the surface in the case of the example just cited, it is somewhat less easy to detect when the challenge takes an apparently more sober form. I wish to claim, however, that the same error underwrites any attempt to turn Quine into a spokesperson for infinite semiosis or a philosopher of untranslatability. 'How do you know that you as a translator mean the exact same thing as the original author when you substitute the word x for his or her word y?' may legitimately solicit the response 'I do not.' It does not, however, follow that we must conclude that we definitely do not mean the same thing as the author when we utter or write the word in question. Nor does this substantive thesis allow us to infer that the quest for synonymy of meaning or reference 'always already' is doomed to failure. An interpretation of Quine's doctrine that in some way involves these kinds of logical slippage amounts to an imprudent scepticism, for it essentially undermines the very possibility of the practice being theorized. Since the term 'translation' presupposes *some* notion of equivalence, any substantive doctrine that dictates the absolute impossibility of synonymy essentially calls for the recognition of the impossibility of the practice in question.[3] In this respect, then, imprudent scepticism is far more devastating than the sceptical challenge to which it responds. For while the sceptical challenge dictates ontological and metaphysical prudence, it does leave large parts of the practice intact. We note, on the other hand, that were the hegemonic publishing houses and teaching institutions to act consequentially upon the claims of the imprudent sceptic, translation according to its more standard definitions would cease to exist. The situation becomes all the more curious when translators *qua* theorists espouse propositions of the imprudent sceptical variety, while continuing to produce their translations within the cognitive and institutional sites where equivalence and synonymy, under some definition thereof, persist as guiding norms and maxims. Such a situation amounts to what Karl-Otto Apel calls a performative self-contradiction, for the axiom being espoused cannot be aligned with the very practice engaged in by the proponent of the allegedly universal principle in question (Apel, 1975). Fortunately, however, such performative self-contradictions do not impose themselves with transcendental necessity, for imprudent scepticism is not the only response to the sceptic's challenge.

Let us now look at the prudent fallibilism which, in my mind, has at least two advantages over the imprudent scepticism just discussed: it follows logically from the sceptical challenge and, just as importantly, it points towards a *pragmatic* definition of the *enabling* conditions of translation. Earlier I claimed, following Kripke, that 'sceptical solutions' to sceptical problems involved showing that the practice in question does not require the kind of justification implied by the sceptic's challenge. Now, Quine's way of posing the problem states that the practice of translation cannot guarantee synonymy of privately intended meanings. Yet Quine himself provides a sceptical solution to this dilemma in his emphasis on regulative maxims and conceptual schemata that are instantiated, not at the level of a single individual, but in bodies of explicitly articulated and publicly available theories. The solution does not admit the possibility of proving that a given translation captures the 'real' meanings of an original text, in the mentalist or idealist sense of the meanings intended by the author. It does, however, allow for a correct translation, the criteria of correctness being a matter of satisfying appropriateness conditions and intersubjectively mediated rules or norms.

What we may learn from the sceptic is that metaphysical categories cannot ground our practices as translators. We cannot prove that linguistic meaning exists independently of the individuating activity of agents operating within the limits established by their conceptual schemata. It is impossible to prove the existence of an exact identity relation between the conceptual schemata pertaining to speakers of the same language, let alone those speaking different tongues. As a result the norm that grounds a translation and serves as its yardstick of success cannot be that of a wholly exact rendering of an author's intended meanings in a target language. Yet perfect fidelity, as defined along these essentialist and mentalist lines, is not necessarily a constitutive feature of translations that satisfy the socially defined norms of correctness and appropriateness. Indeed, in order to produce a correct translation, one in harmony with public norms and conventions, a translator is sometimes obliged to diverge quite radically from what may be inferred about the author's intentions. Take the example of sexist language. In the guidelines set forth in a pamphlet called 'Preparation of Manuscript and Illustrations', the editors of Cornell University Press include the following clause on sexist language: 'the Press asks that you avoid the use of sexual stereotypes and the implication, through use of insensitive language, that either sex is confined to specific roles and occupations.' Many are the non-Anglophone authors known to espouse sexist and antiquated views, who, in this respect, have been presented to North American audiences as socially correct. Correctness here is measured in terms of a harmony between the translated text and social norms and *not* by an equivalence of meaning between the source text and translation. This same point is supported by the particular functions that North

American presses delegate to copy-editors. A translator operating according to mentalist norms will typically find him or herself thwarted by individuals charged with *standardizing* style, syntax, vocabulary, punctuation, and so on. So much for the idea that translations are always effectively governed by the maxim that the translation should reproduce the author's style in all of its minute specificity.

The pragmatic success, then, of a translation is determined by the extent to which it accords with certain social, political and linguistic conventions. This emphasis on conventions does not, however, wed us to some unrealistic and simplistic view defining translation as a mechanical substitution of words following explicit rules. What we need, then, is a definition of a convention that allows us to explain the following two points: (1) how it is that notions of better and worse continue to impinge on our practices as translators; and (2) how it is that a translator's product can be deemed good or bad, even in the absence of wholly explicit transformational rules. David Lewis' attempt to define conventions in terms of common knowledge is particularly useful in this respect. What, then, are the main points of Lewis' definition?[4] Following Lewis, conventions emerge as arbitary solutions to co-ordination problems. They are based on common knowledge and on a preference to have one's behaviour conform to that of others, on a preference, that is, for co-ordination. Common knowledge involves a potentially infinite series of loop beliefs of the following kind: I know that you know that I know that you know that I know ... that x. Conventions may, but need not, be explicit. In other words, common knowledge may result from inferences about recurrent patterns of behaviour. In my mind, Lewis' definition is of interest in relation to translation precisely because it leaves room for implicit norms and social expectations. No dictionary legislates that Freud's use of the word *Trieb* should be translated as 'drive' as opposed to 'instinct', and many give both terms as possible synonyms for the German term. A translator, however, who is informed about the history of Freud translation knows that he or she will be expected to follow certain conventions in translating this term. An informed translator who renders *Trieb* as 'driving force' or 'sexual urge' without justifying this divergence from a particular instance of common knowledge knows that he or she will probably be considered incompetent. With this example we begin to move away from explicit and univocal rules into the zone of the implicit, with all of its possibilities for contradiction, false attribution and so on.

A pragmatic theory of translation based on the kind of theory of conventions that we have just invoked fits well with the epistemology of prudent fallibilism that emerges from the sceptical arguments against classical, foundationalist semantics. Such a pragmatic theory observes how the decisions made by translators, their editors and their readers interact in a complex process of reciprocal expectations. At times this process converges on forms of co-ordination, and these equilibria are what were formerly associated with ideas of 'faithfulness' and 'accuracy' in the rendering of meaning. But there is no guarantee that this kind of co-ordination will always be achieved, or that it will really have the perfection dreamt of in the classical theories. Conventions fail, change, and are anything but binding, for they operate without any transcendent anchor. But to see that conventional practices are fallible does not mean that they always fail, which is why we should reject the imprudent conclusions that are being proclaimed by a certain vein of scepticism, for which meaning is only a drift.

Notes

1. In 'Ontological Relativity' Quine explicitly states that 'radical translation begins at home'. He subsequently goes on to provide an example of how inscrutability of reference and indeterminacy of meaning may pervade our everyday encounters and exchanges: 'Must we equate our neighbor's English words with the same strings of phonemes in our own mouths? Certainly not; for sometimes we do not thus equate them. Sometimes we find it to be in the interests of communication to recognize that our neighbor's use of some word, such as "cool" or "square" or "hopefully" differs from ours, and so we translate that word of his into a different string of phonemes in our idiolect' (Quine, 1969: 46).
2. For admirable efforts along these lines, see Davidson (1973–4).
3. For a bibliography on the issue of equivalence in translation, the reader may usefully consult part one of Susan Bassnett-McGuire's *Translation Studies* (1980).
4. The more technical definition, as given by Lewis, reads as follows:

   A regularity R in the behaviour of a population P when they are agents in a recurrent situation S is a *convention* if and only if it is true that, and it is common knowledge in P that, in almost any instance of S among members of P,
   (1) almost everyone conforms to R;
   (2) almost everyone expects almost everyone else to conform to R;
   (3) almost everyone has approximately the same preferences regarding all possible combinations of actions;
   (4) almost everyone prefers that any one more conform to R, on condition that almost everyone conform to R;
   (5) almost everyone would prefer that any one more conform to R', on condition that almost everyone conform to R',
   where R' is some possible regularity in the behaviour of members of P is S, such that almost no one in almost any instance of S among members of P could conform both to R' and to R. (Lewis, 1986: 78)

References

Apel, Karl-Otto (1975) 'The Problem of Philosophical Fundamental-Grounding in Light of a Transcendental Pragmatic of Language', *Man and World* 8: 239–75.

Bassnett-McGuire, Susan (1980) *Translation Studies*. London and New York: Methuen.

Davidson, Donald (1973–4) 'On the Very Idea of a Conceptual Scheme', *Proceedings and Addresses of the American Philosophical Association* 47: 5–20.

Davidson, Donald (1984) 'The Inscrutability of Reference', in *Inquiries into Truth and Interpretation*. Oxford: Clarendon Press: 227–41.

Di Virgilio, Paul Samuel (1984) 'The Sense of a Beginning: The Dynamics of Context in Translation', *Meta* 29: 115–27.

Hintikka, Jaakko and Davidson, Donald (eds) (1969) *Words and Objections: Essays on the Work of W.V. Quine*. Dordrecht: D. Reidel.

Kripke, Saul A. (1982) *On Rules and Private Language: An Elementary Exposition*. Cambridge, MA: Harvard University Press.

Lewis, David (1986) *Convention: A Philosophical Study*. Oxford: Basil Blackwell.

Morris, Charles (1938) *Foundations of the Theory of Signs*. Chicago and London: University of Chicago Press.

Norris, Christopher (1983) *The Deconstructive Turn: Essays in the Rhetoric of Philosophy*. London: Methuen.

Quine, Willard van Orman (1960) *Word & Object*. Cambridge, MA: MIT Press.

Quine, Willard van Orman (1969) 'Ontological Relativity', in *Ontological Relativity and Other Essays*. New York: Columbia University Press: 26–68.

Smith, Peter (1981) *Realism and the Progress of Science*. Cambridge: Cambridge University Press.

4 Translation in Oral Tradition as a Touchstone for Translation Theory and Practice

Maria Tymoczko

The theory of translation is inseparable from its history; as with any empirical endeavour, concrete data are at the base of theoretical formulation and model construction for translation. Recent work on the history of translation has documented the ways in which translation is a form of literary refraction: translated texts are processed texts, texts that are manipulated as they move between literary systems. Theoretical formulations, in turn, have made sense of those literary interfacings, illuminating the sociological, ideological and literary constants at work behind the manipulations involved in translation (Even-Zohar, 1978; Toury, 1980; Lefevere and Jackson, 1982; Herman, 1985).

Despite the historical documentation and theoretical formulation built up over more than a decade now, the idea that translation necessarily involves manipulation – ideological and poetic processing – remains shocking to traditionalists, students and teachers alike, who persist in the belief in a value-free translation process. The historical examples mustered, no matter how old or how culturally diverse, are seen somehow as yet another sign of the perversity of the modern age: in the lost golden age preceding this rusty iron one, translation would surely have been a pure process.

Since evidence about translation between literate societies overwhelmingly supports theoretical models suggesting that translation involves interpretation and adaptation conditioned by such factors as ideology and poetics, if we are to look for a 'golden age of pure translation' presumably we must find such forms of translation in cultures that are oral or pre-literate. The purpose of this paper is to assess the phenomenon of interlingual literary translation in oral cultures and the phenomenon of literary translation under conditions influenced by the literary practices of oral cultures. Three cases will be considered: oral translation of a fixed literary text, oral translation of oral multiforms (where there is no fixed text), and written translation of oral source texts in circumstances influenced by traditional oral aesthetics including oral variation.[1]

One of the most amusing and yet most revealing documents about an oral translation of a fixed literary text is Laura Bohannan's account of her attempt to translate the story of *Hamlet* in West Africa in 1966 to a group of illiterate tribal elders. Bohannan's account is so rich, one is tempted to quote it *in extenso*; but as that is impossible, we must consider the matter in a schematized form here. On a cold, rainy morning Bohannan was pressed to tell a tale of the 'things of long ago' of her country; she chose to translate *Hamlet* because she saw the tale as 'universally intelligible' (1966: 28–9). She believed that human nature was 'pretty much the same the whole world over' and that 'at least the general plot and motivation of the greater tragedies would always be clear – everywhere – although some details of custom might have to be explained and difficulties of translation might produce other slight changes' (1966: 28).

We can note first that, in the oral context, *Hamlet* was translated in a summary fashion rather than line by line, much less word by word. Thus, for example, Hamlet's soliloquy was omitted when Bohannan discovered that the value system of the receptor culture caused severe interference in understanding Hamlet's motivations and concerns. In translating *Hamlet* Bohannan also automatically adopted the oral formulas of the receptor culture; as she puts it, 'I began in the proper style, "Not yesterday, not yesterday, but long ago, a thing occurred"' (1966: 29). Without hesitation she also transposed Shakespeare's tale to the material culture of the receptor system: Hamlet speaks with his mother in her 'sleeping hut', and Hamlet and Laertes fight with machetes. At times in her oral translation she used English borrowings for concepts not shared by the receptor system: *ghost* had to remain since the audience 'didn't believe in the survival after death of any individuating part of the personality' and hence had no equivalent term (1966: 30). At other times Bohannan took the closest lexical equivalent; *scholar* became 'a man who knew things', a term synonymous with *witch* (1966: 29).

These adaptations did not begin to suffice. The audience objected that Hamlet had no business being the principal in the investigation of the 'omen' of the father's ghost since the task should properly fall to the 'dead chief's' brother (1966: 29). Similarly they failed to understand why Ophelia's chastity should be of concern to her father since whatever she might lose in brideprice by becoming Hamlet's mistress, 'a chief's son would give his mistress's father enough presents and patronage to more than make up the difference'; they concluded that Polonius was a fool, thus accidentally converging on European judgement of the character as well (1966: 31). Her audience also took Bohannan to task for not understanding the genealogical details of the story: she was instructed that the genealogical details would make all the difference in the meaning of the story and that when she returned home she must ask her elders whether Claudius and Hamlet's father were full brothers or only half-brothers. Finally, as she was translating the story, the audience informed Bohannan that madness could be caused solely by a witchspell cast by relatives in the male line, a point that had immediate though not fully obvious implications for the thematic reception of the story.

But the real problems of transposing the elementary core of *Hamlet* became clear to Bohannan only when the audience approved of Claudius's marrying Gertrude a month after the funeral, with one member of the audience commenting to the rest 'He did well . . . I told you that if we knew more about Europeans, we would find they were really very like us' (1966: 29). Indeed they objected to the very idea that Gertrude should mourn longer, lest she have no one to hoe her farms after the death of her husband. Bohannan was faced with an audience that believed that a brother should marry the chief wife of his dead brother soon after the man's death and, hence, that 'Claudius and Gertrude had behaved in the best possible manner' (1966: 30).

The long and short of Bohannan's account is that eventually the audience itself began to take over the telling of the story. They warmed to the task, aided by the contents of a circulating calabash, and began to advance motivations for the characters based on expectations generated by the values of the receptor culture and their own cultural belief in witchcraft (e.g. 'only witches can make people drown' 1966: 33). They eventually told her,

You tell the story well, and we are listening. But it is clear that the elders of your country have never told you what the story really means. No, don't interrupt! We believe you when you say your marriage customs are different, or your clothes and weapons. But people are the same everywhere; therefore, there are always witches and it is we, the elders, who know how witches work. (1966: 33)

The audience advanced various interpretations in their efforts to understand the story. Bohannan reports that after one such interpretation, 'There was a murmur of applause. *Hamlet* was again a good story to them, but *it no longer seemed quite the same story to me*' (1966: 32; my emphasis).

The tribesmen decided that Laertes had killed Ophelia by witchcraft so that he might sell her body to witches, thereby paying the gambling debts he had incurred in Paris; the reason Laertes had jumped into her grave was to retrieve Ophelia's body, nobly resisted in this attempt by Hamlet. And Hamlet, bewitched by his uncle Claudius, ironically had become mad enough to raise his hand against his father's brother, even though no man might use violence against his senior relatives. The audience congratulated Bohannan for telling a good story with 'very few mistakes', and invited her to tell them other stories so that, as they put it, 'we who are elders, will instruct you in their true meaning, so that when you return to your own land your elders will see that you have not been sitting in the bush, but among those who know things and who have taught you wisdom' (1966: 33).

Bohannan's article illustrates in an immediate and specific manner the conditions of translation in an oral context; her account is particularly striking since it concerns the translation of a work that for most of us is so paradigmatically text-based and determinate. The conditions of translation in oral or pre-literate cultures usually preclude the sort of record Bohannan has provided, since rarely in an oral context is there any literate recorder to capture the process for posterity. But the same parameters documented by Bohannan in the specific case of translating *Hamlet* in West Africa are writ large and confirmed implicitly by the overall record of transfer and translation ('translation' in both the literal and etymological senses) of oral folk narratives in other contexts.

The most striking thing about any family of cultures is the sharing of certain narrative sequences, narrative sequences that are generally referred to as 'tale types'.[2] It is apparent, for example, that the tale type called by folklorists 'The Dragon Slayer' is found all over the Indo-European culture area; tales like 'Cinderella' or 'The Magic Flight' exist in most European nations irrespective of language. Early views of the diffusion and transfer of folk-tales naively posited a ripple or stream effect involving the translation of stories from the centres where the stories were initially invented, thus explaining the common occurrence of such tale types throughout a wide cultural area.

The case of *Hamlet* in West Africa, however, illustrates resistance to the translation and transfer of concepts ('ghost'), values ('chastity' of Ophelia), customs (the European period of mourning), motivations (Hamlet's madness), material culture (swords for machetes), and plot sequence, as well as rhetorical and linguistic structures. The awareness of such resistance to the uptake and translation of oral material, as well as a better understanding of the actual working dynamic between passive and active bearers of traditional cultures, has led to re-evaluations of the process of survival, transmission and translation of oral literature.

Various sorts of barrier affect the transmission of oral literary traditions including geographical, political, religious and linguistic boundaries. Von Sydow has stressed the difficulties in the successful transfer of folk-tales and folk culture in most circumstances, suggesting that in general where there is cultural interface because of travel, migration or shared boundaries, transmission simply does not occur. He cites a variety of reasons for the breakdown in transmission: stories cannot function because the social, kinship, or geographical grounding of the material does not exist; active bearers of tradition become passive bearers in the absence of suitable audiences; and so forth (Von Sydow, 1948: 18–21). Thus, where we find common narrative patterns, Von Sydow attributes them usually to a common heritage – to, for example, the survival of a pre-Indo-European narrative, or a shared Indo-European inheritance, or the common literary tradition of a more restricted culture group such as the Celts (1948: 55 ff.). Indeed, for a tale to succeed in a new cultural milieu, he stresses that it will 'adapt itself more and more to prevailing taste, becoming fully acclimatised' (1948: 52). The result is an *oicotype*, differing considerably 'from that of the country of origin' (1948: 52), where by *oicotype* Von Sydow means a special form of a tale type that is a local development and that is characteristic of a particular area (Thompson, 1946: 440–3).

When we look at the different versions of an oral tale type coming from a variety of linguistic communities, we, like Bohannan, are struck by how different 'the same tale' commonly is. Ireland's 'Cinderella' is a servant girl aided by her dead mother come back in the form of a cat; the girl meets her 'prince' at a fair. In Greek tales Mediterranean flora and fauna replace the dense woods of the tales of northern Europe. Plot sequences develop particularized configurations in particular areas. The formulaic openings and closings, catchphrases, modes of description – the grammar of the traditional rhetoric – are distinct in every oral tradition. Such examples could be multiplied. It is clear even from a cursory examination that in oral traditions international tale types adapt to local conditions (including sociological, geographical, historical and lingusitic conditions) and local tastes (including aesthetic and rhetorical tastes); tale types become 'fully acclimatised'. We must conclude, therefore, that 'pure translation' is not a feature of the transmission of oral literature; this is the inductive conclusion that follows from a broad survey of oral folk materials as well as from particular examples such as that of Bohannan.

The same conclusions are supported by translations of oral materials into written texts when such translations are undertaken in a context influenced by the standards of oral literature. There are many medieval translations that could serve as examples here, but perhaps the most striking of them is Geoffrey of Monmouth's *Historia Regum*

Britanniae, 'The History of the Kings of Britain'. The work dates from c.1136; it was addressed to Robert Earl of Gloucester and King Stephen of England, and it served as a summary of the Celtic history of Britain for the new Norman royal house of England. Geoffrey's sources included some written documents – including a collection of Welsh pedigrees and the Latin works of Gildas and Bede – but it is generally agreed that for the most part his sources were oral (Loomis, 1959: 81). Geoffrey's use of Latin for his work which marks him as a member of the literate clerical classes does not mean he was divorced from the standards of oral translation. Since all the vernacular cultures of Britain, whether English, Viking, Welsh or Norman, were cultures in which literature was primarily oral, Geoffrey was inevitably influenced by oral practice; moreover, the very enterprise in which he engaged – the preservation and translation of Welsh oral historical tradition – shows that he valued oral vernacular literature. Geoffrey was also addressing patrons whose literary sensibilities were formed primarily by an oral aesthetic.

In evaluating Geoffrey's translation of Welsh oral stories into written Latin narrative, we must again proceed inferentially, for by virtue of the fact that they were oral we have lost Geoffrey's actual sources. We must judge his procedures by comparing *The History of the Kings of Britain* with surviving written narratives from medieval Wales, and with other written materials in Latin. The conclusions of such a comparison can in this context be presented only in summary fashion, rather than through detailed textual analysis. Briefly, Geoffrey's Welsh oral sources were likely to have been relatively short heroic tales, involving native values, customs and social standards (the standards of a tribal culture), possibly having a mixed narrative tone including humour, burlesque, sexual or scatological materials, as well as epic elements. The Welsh narratives were also ultimately based on a native mythic substratum.

Geoffrey translates these materials into a Latin genre – historical chronicle – with a Latin literary aesthetic. His Latin historiography shapes his presentation of time, space and causality in his narrative. Influenced in part by the Latin epic tradition, the *Aeneid* in particular, Geoffrey introduces speeches that draw on Latin rhetorical and oratorical principles; and he manages battle scenes in ways that show the influence of Latin epic as well. Along with his choice of genre and rhetorical conventions, he also introduces certain narrative motifs and sequences into the Welsh materials; we find, for example, the motif of *fortuna* and the plotting theme of the letter, where the originals would have had an implicit fatalism and the theme of the messenger.

Geoffrey manipulates values as well. Most of the Welsh oral historical materials of his time – particularly those pertaining to Arthur – show primarily a heroic value system. Geoffrey manipulates the heroic values of his source materials with the result that his characters are motivated by a value system closer to contemporary values of the Francophone world than to the values of Welsh heroic literature. Thus, the ideas of moderation, compassion and mercy are more in evidence than they are in Welsh Arthurian materials; honour gives way to the notion that 'there is nothing better or more enjoyable than life itself';[3] and the importance of Christianity and the moral imperative of resisting the pagan enemies, themes that are characteristic of French epic, are introduced.

Geoffrey is conscious of his role as translator. Though he depends on Welsh onomastic and genealogical materials, Welsh concepts of geography, and the Welsh love of triads, he makes all his materials accessible to his receptor audience. He adds details and circumstantiality that the native oral materials lack, taking care to introduce his characters and to situate them spatially or temporally, so as to assure that the materials would be comprehensible to his Norman audience which was unfamiliar with the traditional Welsh oral historical background.

The History of the Kings of Britain can also be said to be 'de-Celticized' in some respects. Names are changed to make the phonology more palatable to a Norman audience – the most famous of these changes is Geoffrey's change of the name *Myrddin* to *Merlinus*, presumably to avoid homophony with the French *merde*. In Geoffrey's narrative Arthur becomes a king where in Welsh tradition he was either *ameraudur*, 'emperor', or simply a tribal leader. Some native customs are attenuated – the Celtic customs, for example, of fosterage and tribute. Instead Norman customs are introduced; primogeniture is stressed, and there are references to feudal obligations. Moreover, in Geoffrey's account Roman mythological figures replace Germanic or Celtic pagan deities.

These adaptations indicate that Geoffrey's translation is intended to be an acceptable translation rather than an adequate one; it is oriented to the target culture rather than to the source culture. The result is that Geoffrey made Welsh oral history intelligible to the readers of his translation; indeed he made it possible for *The History of the Kings of Britain* to be singularly memorable to his Norman audience and beyond to a wider European community. That he was successful is shown by the number of manuscript copies of his work that have come down to us, by the great number of translations of Geoffrey's work into European vernaculars (ironically including several back translations into Welsh), and by the development of Arthurian romance which is demonstrably indebted to his seminal work.

Geoffrey stands as but one example of a medieval translator adopting translation procedures that grow out of an oral aesthetic about literary adaptation and translation. We could do a similar analysis of works of Marie de France and other specific writers of the period, as well as of many anonymous saints' lives, romances, *lais*, and historical materials. In most of these cases we see strategies that are radically oriented to the requirements of the target audience and that, thus, result in the dramatic refraction and manipulation of the source materials.

To summarize, then, whether we look at interlingual oral translations of written or fixed literary texts, interlingual oral translations of oral literary materials, or written translations of oral literature done in cultural contexts dominated by the standards of an oral aesthetic, we find similar translation procedures. Translation in oral tradition involves the adaptation of narrative to the poetics and ideology of the target culture. In oral tradition translated narrative is naturalized to the natural and social context and to the ideology of the receptor culture. Translation in oral tradition also involves adaptation to the poetics and to the 'grammar' of the receptor literary system; translations adopt the motifs, themes, formulas and other structures that make memorable speech possible in the receptor system. In some cases the naturalization of translations in oral tradition even affects the plot sequences of narratives in radical ways.

Several conclusions can be drawn from these investigations. First, it is notable that rarely if ever in discussions of translation theory and practice are there cited examples of interlingual literary translation in oral tradition. Our discussions of the practice and theory of interlingual literary translation generally presuppose the presence of fixed source texts and the generation of fixed translated texts. In ignoring and failing to account for interlingual oral literary translation, the terms of our very discourse about literary translation presuppose a framework about literature and the workings of literature that fails to account for the position of literature in most of the world at present and the position of literature through most of human history.

Such a conceptual presupposition in part accounts for the fixation in translation studies on certain notions about translation that have led to endless and generally irresolvable debate. Thus, the concepts of 'literal' or 'word-for-word' translations, notions which have been part of translation theory since the classical period, depend on literature taking the form of a fixed text; they do not reflect the concerns of literary translation in oral contexts, and indeed they are incompatible with oral literature. To remain alive and to function fully as literature – essentials in oral literary systems – translated narratives *must* adapt to the standards of the receptor culture and hence *must* refract the source text. Translators cannot translate on a 'literal' or 'word-for-word' level; indeed the very notion of 'word' is different in an oral context. When translated literature does not adapt as it does in oral traditions, translated literature becomes antiquarian or exotic. Such literary antiquarianism and exoticism we can hypothesize are born of literacy and are intimately tied to the notion of a fixed text; they are not usually viable in oral traditional cultures. To acknowledge the implication here is to understand immediately the ways in which literate translations of literary texts are imported into the receptor systems for ideological and other cultural purposes.

Western translation standards over the last several hundred years have shown a general drift toward an ideal of 'exactitude' or 'objectivity' in translation, the growth of which can be correlated with the general movement away from oral standards toward text-based literacy in Western culture. The ideal of exactitude has been reinforced and supported by biblical translation, for sacred texts are the paradigmatically fixed texts of a culture. Biblical translation has, thus, served as a standard for translation theory as a whole in Western culture as oral literature has become marginalized and written literature has determined the dominant centre of the literary system. Translation in contexts dominated by oral literary standards reveals that the process of refraction is a regular part of translation; far from presenting us with a standard of exactitude or objectivity, oral literary translations manipulate narrative frankly, radically, unabashedly.

The examples of interlingual literary translation in oral tradition presented here suggest that the dedication to a fixed text – a relatively recent development in human history, and a development still largely restricted worldwide – skews both theoretical and practical notions about translation. Consideration of translation in an oral context shows that extent to which translated literature is normally pulled into the framework of the receptor cultural norms and the receptor literary system. It is our obsession with fixed text that has shifted translation practice over the last two millenia away from oral standards toward types of literalism as Western culture has become increasingly literate and text-based, and increasingly committed to the standard of fixed, written texts, including the fixed text of the Bible. It is important to understand that this development is culture bound, and does not represent any theoretical absolute about literary translation.

Notes

1. For an introduction to the processes of oral tradition and oral multiforms see Thompson, *The Folktale*; Lord, *The Singer of Tales*; and Foley, *The Theory of Oral Composition, History and Method*.
2. Thompson (1946: 415) defines *tale type* in the following manner: 'A type is a traditional tale that has an independent existence. It may be told as a complete narrative and does not depend for its meaning on any other tale.' A listing of Indo-European tale types, including Indo-European wondertales, is found in Aarne and Thompson (1961).

3. *Nichil enim. uita prestantius nichil iocundius* (Geoffrey of Monmouth, 1929: 235 and 1966: 63). We find some analogous value shifts in the four branches of the *Mabinogi*, but elsewhere in eleventh- and twelfth-century Middle Welsh narrative, as it is preserved *in extenso* or as it is reflected in the Welsh Triads, a more heroic tenor is to be found; a heroic value structure is also found in the poetry of the contemporary poets, the *gogynfeirdd*.

References

Aarne, Antti and Stith Thompson (1961) *The Types of the Folktale*. Helsinki: Academia Scientiarum Fennica.

Bohannan, Laura (1966) 'Shakespeare in the Bush', *Natural History* Aug.–Sept.: 28–33.

Even-Zohar, Itamar (1978) *Papers in Historical Poetics*. Tel Aviv: Porter Institute for Poetics and Semiotics.

Foley, John Miles (1988) *The Theory of Oral Composition, History and Method*. Bloomington, IN: Indiana University Press.

Geoffrey of Monmouth (1929) *The 'Historia Regum Britanniae' of Geoffrey of Monmouth*, ed. Acton Griscom. London, New York, Toronto: Longmans, Green.

Geoffrey of Monmouth (1966) *The History of the Kings of Britain*, trans. Lewis Thorpe. Harmondsworth: Penguin Books.

Hermans, Theo (ed.) (1985) *The Manipulation of Literature: Studies in Literary Translation*. London: Croom Helm.

Lefevere, André and K. D. Jackson (eds) (1982) *The Art and Science of Translation*, issued as vol. 7 of *Dispositio*.

Loomis, Roger Sherman (ed.) (1959) *Arthurian Literature in the Middle Ages*. Oxford: Clarendon Press.

Lord, Albert B. (1960) *The Singer of Tales*. Cambridge, MA: Harvard University Press.

Thompson, Stith (1946) *The Folktale*. Berkeley and Los Angeles, CA: University of California Press.

Toury, Gideon (1980) *In Search of a Theory of Translation*. Tel Aviv: Porter Institute of Poetics and Semiotics.

Von Sydow, C. W. (1948) *Selected Papers on Folklore*. Copenhagen: Rosenkilde and Bagger.

5 Translation, Colonialism and Poetics: Rabindranath Tagore in Two Worlds

Mahasweta Sengupta

Discussing the responsibility of a translator to the target-language (TL) audience, Susan Bassnett comments:

To attempt to impose the value-system of the SL [source language] culture onto the TL culture is dangerous ground, and the translator should not be tempted by the school that pretends to determine the original *intentions* of an author on the basis of a self-contained text. The translator cannot *be* the author of the SL text, but as the author of the TL text has a clear moral responsibility to the TL readers. (Bassnett-McGuire, *Studies*, 23)

In this paper I will try to show the consequences of a translator being faithful to the TL audience in a way which ultimately undermines the quality of the translated material and proves to be immensely problematic in the sphere of interlocking cultural values, particularly when these values are part of the colonizer – colonized relationship between the First and Third Worlds.

Let me begin by quoting a poem from Tagore's anthology *Gitanjali: Song Offering* the collection of poems for which he was awarded the Nobel Prize for literature in 1913; it was the first time that the coveted prize was awarded to a non-European, a poet from Asia. In Tagore's own English prose rendering, poem No. 5 reads

I ask for a moment's indulgence to sit by thy side.
The works that I have in hand I will finish afterwards.
Away from the sight of thy face my heart knows no rest or respite, and my work becomes an endless toil in a shoreless sea of toil.
   To-day the summer has come at my window with its sighs and murmurs; and the bees are playing with their ministrelsy at the court of the flowering grove.
   Now it is time to sit quiet, face to face with thee, and to sing dedication of life in this silent and overflowing leisure.
Tagore, *Gitanjali*, 4–5

My literal translation from the original Bengali appears to be considerably different in several respects from this English version in Tagore's prose:

> Let me sit near you only for a little while
> The work I have in my hands,
> I will finish later.
> If I do not look at your face,
> My heart finds no peace;
> The more I plunge myself in work,
> I wander in a sea that has lost its shores.
> Spring with its ecstatic breath
> Has come to my window,
> The lazy bee comes humming
> And dwells in the garden.
> Today it is the time to sit in a nook,
> Look into each other's eyes
> Today the song of life-surrender
> I will sing in the quietness of leisure.

In this example, one can notice clearly that Tagore changes not only the style of the original, but also the imagery and tone of the lyric, not to mention the register of language which is made to match the target-language poetics of Edwardian English. These changes are conscious and deliberately adopted to suit the poetics of the target system, which Tagore does by altering tone, imagery and diction, and as a result, none of the lyrical qualities of the originals are carried over into the English translations.

Why this discrepancy in the form and style of the originals and the translations? Why did Tagore himself choose to render his own poems in a way that was remarkably different from what they were in their original form? These questions take us into the realm of cultural values and the forces that shape our attitudes regarding the 'other'. The case of Tagore clearly illustrates complex factors at work in translation, and proves the problematics of the process in which a translator remains primarily faithful to the audience of the TL culture. This discrepancy in his attitude towards poetry in two different languages has to be examined within the framework of cultural systems and their relationship.

My assumptions regarding the specifically unique nature of the auto-translations of Tagore are based on two distinct premises. The first is that I believe that his understanding of English language and literature was largely influenced by the aesthetic ideology of the Romantic and Victorian periods, the time when imperialism reached its high-water mark in the expansion of the British empire. Though Tagore himself did not have any formal education and heartily disliked the British educational system that was being imposed on India, he nevertheless imbibed the aesthetic ideology that was prevalent at the time of his growing up and learnt the language primarily through its literature. Largely self-taught, he read extensively both English and Sanskrit literatures and translated poems from both languages when he was quite young. In English, he preferred reading Shakespeare, the Romantics and the Victorians. Two remarks made on two different occasions illustrate his ideas and biases towards the English language and its literature.

When we had proceeded well enough in our study of Bangla, we started learning English. Our instructor Aghorbabu was a medical student. He came to teach us in the evening. The discovery of fire is said to be mankind's most important invention, and I do not want to dispute that. But the birds cannot light their homes in the evening, and I cannot but feel how lucky their children are. The language they learn is learnt in the morning and learnt happily. But we should remember that they do not learn English. (Tagore, *Jeevansmiriti*, 22)

Tagore clearly had strong feelings about the imposition of English on youngsters whose minds reacted adversely to the foreign language, and thus early experiences might have shaped his attitude to the culture that this foreign language represented. In a conversation with Edward Thompson much later in his life, Tagore says: 'These new poets of yours speak a new language, and after Keats and Shelley, I cannot understand them. I can understand Blunt and Davies and De la Mare, that is about all'. (Thomson, *Tagore*, 315)

What is apparent is that Tagore deliberately chooses to write like these poets when he translates his own poems into English; he makes adjustments to suit the ideology of the dominating culture or system, and therefore his translations fit the target-language poetics quite easily. He fits perfectly into the stereotypical role that was familiar to the colonizer, a voice that not only spoke of the peace and tranquillity of a distant world, but also offered an escape from the materialism of the contemporary Western world. And here it is that my second assumption regarding the translations of Tagore comes into focus, and I would like to deal with that aspect of the politics of translation in the rest of this paper.

Perhaps the most important fact in this politics is that Tagore himself had chosen a certain class of poems to be rendered into English. These translations were undertaken at a time when the poet was recovering from an illness that made him cancel his third trip to Europe in the spring of 1912, and instead took him to Shelidaha, a district in East Bengal where the Tagores had a family estate and which was a favourite place of his. The new century had been a hard one for Tagore in many respects; his wife and two children had died, he was engrossed in the new experiment of the school he had founded in Santiniketan, but the burden was becoming too heavy for him. In his then state of mind and health, Tagore chose to translate only those poems from several anthologies of verses that were of a particular type – devotional or spiritual. But devotional poems in Bengal and also in India, particularly after the Vaisnava poets, were of a highly ambiguous kind: they talk of the devotee as a lover or a friend and not necessarily as a subject seeking the master. Anyone familiar with the Bengali tradition would have grasped their peculiar appeal: they were both love poems and religious or spiritual poems and derived their imagery largely from Vaisnava literature. This idea certainly did not conform to the orthodox Christian doctrine, and it puzzled Westerners who were unaware of the richness and vitality of that tradition but responded more in terms of the stereotypes that already existed.

My contention is that, in spite of the widely prevalent myth of the sudden and capricious nature of Tagore's efforts at translating his own poems, it could be proved that actually he had been preparing to reach a wider audience for quite some time, and there is a continuous historical process behind the translation of a certain class of poems into English.[1] I believe that these translations could not have been done by anyone other than Tagore himself, because they illustrate the complexity of his venture in the most unique manner. What is striking as well as quite natural is that he approaches poetry in two different languages in two widely different manners. In fact, Tagore inhabits two different worlds when he translates from the originals; in his source language, he is independent and free of the trappings of an alien culture and vocabulary, and writes in the colloquial diction of the actually spoken word. When he translates, he enters another context, a context in which his colonial self finds expression. Tagore illustrates very clearly the validity of the Sapir-Whorf hypothesis that language shapes reality and therefore, when one uses another language, one is entering a different reality. (Sapir, *Culture*, 69)

These translations reached a select audience in England through the efforts of William Rothenstein, who was deeply fascinated by these prose poems. He made three copies from the original and gave them to W. B. Yeats, A. C. Bradley and Stopford Brooke. Yeats read some of these poems at a gathering in Rothenstein's house on 7 July 1912, where visitors included, among others, Ernest Rhys, Evelyn Underhill and C. F. Andrews. Rothenstein also arranged for publication of the translated poems under the title *Gitanjali* or *Song Offering*, initially in a limited edition by the India Society of London, and then by Macmillan. In November of 1913, Tagore was awarded the Nobel Prize for *Gitanjali*.

Immediately after the appearance of the English *Gitanjali*, Tagore became a literary vogue in the West. Yeats had written an introduction to the book, in which he hailed Tagore as a 'saint' who belonged to a 'tradition where poetry and religion are the same thing'. Quite characteristically, Yeats imaginatively recreates what he thinks is the world of Tagore, and muses on its qualities. This is Yeats' 'Other', a world where his imagination and vision find their freedom. He writes:

A whole people, a whole civilization, immeasurably strange to us, seems to have been taken up into this imagination; and yet we are not moved because of its strangeness, but because we have met our own image, as though we had walked in Rossetti's willow woods or heard, for the first time in literature, our voice as in a dream. (Taylor, *Gitanjali*, xvi–xvii)

Yeats also found in these poems a new lease of life, a clarity and simplicity which he had struggled to reach in vain all his life. The previous quotation shows the peculiarly stereotypical quality of the reaction, the wish-fulfilment that is often found in dreams, and dreams that involve Rossetti's willow woods. Yeats goes on to write:

An innocence, a simplicity that one does not find elsewhere in literature makes the birds and leaves seem as near to him as they are near to children, and the changes of the seasons great events as before our thoughts had arisen between them and us. At times I wonder if he has it from the literature of Bengal or from religion, and at other times, . . . I find pleasure in thinking it hereditary, a mystery that was growing through the centuries like the courtesy of a Tristan or a Pelanore. (Taylor, *Gitanjali*, xxi–xxii)

Yeats' reaction was symptomatic of the general appreciation of Tagore in the West, which was largely the product of the confusion between Tagore the poet and Tagore the prophet or mystic from the exotic lands of the East. Researchers have studied the reception of Tagore exhaustively and shown how these translations were being judged on the basis of their mysticism and philosophical content.[2] Most reviewers and critics praised or publicized the translations because of their religious or mystical nature; they were simply repeating the accepted stereotypes of the East then prevalent in the West. The Macmillan Company advertised Tagore's translated works in accordance with the general feeling in the West. A few examples will illustrate the way they were reading Tagore's poems:

Here is the kernel of the wisdom and insight of the great Hindu seer in the form of short extracts. These sayings are largely taken from his other works, and are the essence of his Eastern message to the Western world.

Notice the words 'wisdom', 'seer', 'sayings', 'Eastern message' – they are indicative of the general reaction to the translations. Tagore, the avant-garde artist in Bengali, was represented as a saint or a seer from the East, a seer who was bringing the message of peace and spirituality to strife-torn, pre-1914 Europe.

Perhaps the most fascinating piece of evidence regarding the colonial encounter comes from the citation of the Nobel Prize, where the Nobel Committee refers to *Gitanjali* as 'a collection of religious poems'. (Frenz, *Nobel*, 127) This document is a wonderful proof of the attitude of the West towards a poet from the East who was being judged for his ability to transmit wisdom and not because of his artistic abilities. My assumption is that this is the only way in which the colonizer was prepared to deal with the colonized, the only possible ground for admitting one from the subject race, who is accepted because he represents the wisdom and exoticism of the 'other' world. Tagore's mission in the West became something very different from that of an artist or poet, and his poetry in translation became a vehicle for his mission.

At first, there was controversy within the Nobel Committee regarding the selection of someone from such a 'distant location' (whatever that meant); then this problem was resolved by mentioning the 'express wish and desire that, in the awarding of the prize, no consideration should be paid to the nationality to which any proposed candidate might belong.' (Frenz, *Nobel*, 127) The question of nationality was an important one, but since the prize was after all being given to a British subject, there was not much to lose by mentioning that.

The committee solved this dilemma: 'We do know, however, that the poet's motivation extends to the effort of reconciling two spheres of civilization widely separated' (Frenz, *Nobel*, 128).

Yet the committee did not fail to add the most important item on the agenda:

The true inwardness of this work is most clearly and purely revealed in the efforts exerted in the Christian mission-field throughout the world. ... Thanks to this movement, bubbling springs of living water have been tapped, from which poetry in particular may draw inspiration, even though those springs are perhaps mingled with alien streams, and whether or not they be traced to the depths of the dreamworld. More especially, the preaching of the Christian religion has provided in many places the first definite impulse toward a revival and regeneration of the vernacular language, i.e., its liberation from the bondage of an artificial tradition, and consequently also toward a development of its capacity for nurturing and sustaining a vein of living and natural poetry. (Frenz, *Nobel*, 129)

The reason why I quote so extensively from the citation is because it appears to me as an extremely important testimony of cultural imperialism, a document which extends and approves the hegemony of the colonizing culture by naturalizing the native poet as a part of, or an extension of, the Christian mission-field in Asia.

It is obvious that the West was prepared to accept the poet Tagore only on two distinct grounds, as a mystic or a religious prophet, and as a person who was following the Christian missionaries in their task of unshackling the natives from the bondage of tradition and history. The irony remains that Tagore himself had provided the basis for such an appraisal by translating his works in a manner that suited the psyche of the colonizer, a manner that was perfectly adjusted to the prevailing paradigms of the East. The poet and his poetry were lost in this politics of translation. Mysticism was a highly prized virtue during the first decades of the twentieth century, and Tagore was conveniently categorized as a type, a type that he helped create through his translations.

The last important idea in the citation sums up this attitude quite well. The poem quoted in this paper proves that not all poems in *Gitanjali* were overtly spiritual or religious, and there are others which contain a wide variety of emotions and tones. The Nobel Citation, however, generalizes on the basis of the common assumptions about the wisdom of the East and says:

Praise, prayer, and fervent devotion pervade the song-offerings that he lays at the feet of this nameless divinity of his. Ascetic and even ethic austerity would appear to be alien to this type of divinity worship, which may be characterized as a species of aesthetic theism. Piety of that description is in full concord with the whole of his poetry, and it has bestowed peace upon him. He proclaims the coming of that peace for weary and careworn souls even within the bounds of Christendom. (Frenz, *Nobel*, 132)

Tagore, therefore, was valuable because he was capable of bestowing peace on weary and unhappy souls, even among the Christians. As a matter of fact, *Gitanjali* fell so easily into the Western stereotype of Eastern mysticism that other aspects of the work were completely ignored.

Tagore's reputation and immense popularity in the West in the first three decades of this century were not based on an intellectual appreciation of his works but on the emotional association of the East as an enigma, where saints and prophets brought deliverance to ordinary people. In other words, Tagore was supplying another basis for the already existing superstructure of orientalism; he became a representative of the alluring 'Other' to the Western world. He became a missionary with a difference, but a missionary none the less, through his translations.

It is quite natural and obvious that Tagore's reputation did not survive the onslaughts of time in the West. He was forgotten as fast as he was made famous; very soon, the West found him immensely boring and discarded him as a passing vogue. Western literati were now wary and intolerant of the same qualities for which they had exalted Tagore a few years earlier. The war and consequent happenings had changed the West's aesthetic ideology about poetry.

English poetics was becoming professedly modern, and the revolt against Romanticism, Victorianism and Edwardianism was the slogan of the avant-garde. Tagore's translations were the victim of this change in poetics and ideology, which was just a manifestation of the deep-rooted change in the life and time of the Western audience. Moreover, Tagore also proved to be very different from what the colonizer had thought him to be. He was vehemently lecturing against nationalism in its fierce forms, and in so doing created enemies both at home and abroad. He was growing out of the straitjacket the West had cut for a poet from the East.

Reviews and articles consequently started pouring out their unabashed criticism of his works – the exact opposite of the ovation they had offered him a few years before. Rabindranath Tagore lived until 1941, and he remained an innovator in his creative efforts throughout his life. His writings in Bengali changed the course of that literature and also influenced the life and literatures of the subcontinent. He is a vital influence even now in Bengal and in India and represents the cultural achievements of the people in many ways. In English translation, however, we get a very different Tagore, a writer who is epigonic and tied to an ideology associated with colonialism and cultural domination, where his poems speak in terms of the master–servant relationship. His overt faithfulness to the target-language audience has proved to be devastating for his works in translation.

Notes

1. In a recent article in *Pratikshan* (Calcutta, 1986), Bikash Chakravarti shows the process of the preparation for Tagore's debut in the West with his auto-translations. Complete citation of this article was not available to me at the time of writing.
2. Nabaneeta Devsen deals exhaustively with Tagore's reception in the West in her dissertation *The Reception of Tagore in England, France and Germany and the United States* (Indiana University, 1963) as does Sujit Kumar Mukherjee in his dissertation *Passage to America: The Reception of Tagore in the United States 1912–41* (University of Pennsylvania, 1963).

References

Bassnett-McGuire, Susan (1980) *Translation Studies*. London: Methuen.
Frenz, Horst Ed. (1969) *Nobel Lectures on Literature*. London: Nobel Foundation.
Sapir, Edward (1956) *Culture, Language and Personality*. Berkeley & Los Angeles: University of California Press.
Tagore, Rabindranath (1915) *Gitanjali*. New York: Macmillan.
Tagore, Rabindranath (1961) "Jeevansmriti." *Complete Works*. Vol. 10. Calcutta: Govenment of West Bengal, 15 vols.
Thompson, Edward (1926) *Rabindranath Tagore: Poet and Dramatist*. London: Oxford University Press.

6 Culture as Translation

Vladimír Macura

In 1832 John Bowring published in London a relatively voluminous anthology of Czech poetry under the Czech–English title: *Wýbor z básnictwi českého, Cheskian Anthology: Being a History of the Poetical Literature of Bohemia with Translated Specimens*. At that time Bowring, an enthusiast for exotic and godforsaken places on the map of European culture, a bankrupt businessman, then and later in the foreign service of the British government, already had a number of similar publications to his credit: two editions of the anthology *Rossijkaya antologgiya, Specimens of the Russian Poets* (1820, 1821), *Batavian Anthology* (1824), *Wybór z poezyi polskiéy, Specimens of the Polish Poets* (1827), *Poetry of the Magyars. Preceded by a Sketch of the Language and Literature of Hungary and Transylvania* (1830).

John Bowring translated to express his enchantment with the number and variety of the cultures of this world. In the introduction to his Hungarian volume we read: 'In Europe, at least, there are no moral or intellectual wildernesses. Let others go forth with me to gather its fruits and flowers' (Bowring, 1830: viii). But he also mythologized his mission from another point of view. Translation into English was for him a medium to bring lesser-known cultural areas into the full light of Western civilization: 'Say to Hungaria, she shall stand among/the lands which Poetry with glory girds . . . (Bowring, 1830: ix). In fact, Bowring's attempts at translation did not and could not evoke any greater interest on the part of the English audience in the smaller, darker corners of the continent of Europe. His translations have to be viewed above all as curiosa, both in language and in subject matter. John Bowring took great pleasure in introducing extensive quotations from various source languages into his translations and in providing his books with exotic titles containing the languages he translated from. A certain ironic approach to the audience was suggested by a parody of Bowring's style published in 1830 in *Fraser's Magazine*:

Te pikke megge

Hogy, wogy, Pogy!
Xupumxé trtzaa bnikttm;
Pogy, wogy, hogy!
Bsdrno plglvz cttnsttm;
Wogy hogy Pogy!
Mlerz wbquogp fvikktm

the 'translation' of which reads as follows:

The Pious Maiden

Holy little Polly!
Love sought me, but I tricked him.
Polly, little holy!
You thought of me, 'I've nick'd him!'
Little holy Polly!
I'm not to be your victim.

(Churchill and Maginn, 1830: 434)

On the other hand, it was necessary to fight for the values of cultures on their home ground. The poet František Ladislav Čelakovský wrote to his friend and fellow poet Kamaryt with enthusiasm about Browning's plan to publish a translation of Czech poetry: 'Imagine, we shall come as far as America and there we shall be known, even though we are unknown in our native country' (Čelakovský, 1865: 207). The sentence reflects enthusiasm, but there is also a bitter kernel of truth concealed in all the ostentatious euphoria. The awareness of the contradiction between Bowring's effort to show Czech literature as a fact of world culture and the Czechs seeing it as an experiment with doubtful results also predetermined the change from initial euphoria to quick disenchantment. The enthusiasm did not even outlast the five years that elapsed between the hatching of the first plans for the anthology and its actual date of print.

Bowring's efforts in this area were condemned by merciless Time to become so many curiosa, both from the English point of view and from the point of view of the nations whose literature he translated. Yet one substantial aspect should be remembered. For John Bowring translation meant above all an act of cultural information. Characteristically, he preferred the anthology, taking advantage of all the possibilities this type of publication is able to marshal for a more complex 'modelling' of foreign literature and culture. Bowring's fascination with this 'genre' also manifested iself in the criticism he published in the *Foreign Quarterly Review* and the *Westminster Review*. The anthology allowed him to bring together individual translated poems as sign-indexes pointing to the original totality and providing information about it. It further allowed for the incorporation of different data about authors and could constitute a dictionary of the writers of a given area. Finally, it also sanctioned supplementing the volume of poetry with a sketch of the development of a national literature and with encyclopaedic information about the language and history of the region. The book of translations conceived as an anthology was not designed to mediate unique aesthetic values; it functioned primarily as a sign whose *signifié* was a culture as such.

From this perspective, Bowring's 'Cheskian' anthology seems to give a relatively precise idea of Czech culture and particularly literature at the beginning of the nineteenth century, the time of the national revival (Macura, 1983). It also reveals a great many distinctive features of the epoch which were obscured and concealed by later developments, and can therefore be used as an interesting document on the characterology of the Czech revival, the more so because the book was compiled in co-operation with Czech intellectuals, most obviously Čelakovský, (see p. 64 and Beer, 1904), and therefore adopted their opinions, their attitudes, their systems of values – in short the whole of what Robert Burton Pynsent has called the 'Revivalist mythopoeia' (Pynsent, 1988: 64). By including a segment of the national poetry, the Cheskian anthology demonstrates the prestige of folklore art in nascent Czech culture. Incorporation of the poet Karel Šnajdr (Schneider) reflects cases of the 'Czechisation' of Germans and of winning them over to the programme of the Czech-speaking culture. The book also involuntarily reveals a strong tendency towards mystification at the time of the Revival, as well as the blurred boundaries between playfulness and seriousness deriving from the necessity to create a Czech culture 'here and now', as a complete structure with a fully developed past.

The illusion of that past was created with the help of literary forgeries, such as the Dvŏr Králové, abundantly quoted by Bowring. Czech culture also needed a fully developed present: the ideal of a woman poetess, unachievable at the time, was to materialize in the fictive poetess Žofie Jandová, whose poetry Bowring included bona fide, evidently on the recommendation of Čelakovský, who was the real author of her poems, even though the forgery had been exposed in Bohemia in 1823, nearly ten years before the publication of the Cheskian anthology in England, and about four years before the first contact between Čelakovský and Bowring took place in correspondence.

Today Bowring's translations strike us as a true 'copy' of Czech Revivalist culture, maybe also because of the exclusive position translation occupied in that culture. By this I do not mean the high number of translations in the literary production of that time, but the explicit translation-like character of the whole culture as such, the unmistakable structural homology which exists between Czech revivalist culture and translation. Bowring's 'translation as culture', the translation which is a model of a culture, coalesced in a happy alliance – though unperceived as such by contemporaries – with 'culture as translation', or 'translation-like culture', i.e. a culture which more or less accepts the structure of translation. The ideal of Czech culture which prevailed in Bohemia in the first decades of the nineteenth century was based on the quick, immediate formation of a well stratified, complex cultural production, able to satisfy all the needs of a modern, socially differentiated society – even at the price of the non-existence of a corresponding socially differentiated Czech society, which would not come into being for a few more decades yet.

The idea of Czech culture as a complex system presupposed the creation of literature, journalism, theatre, science, by analogy to the cultures of contemporary developed Europe. Under the prevailing historical conditions this meant that no emphasis would or could be given to the originality of cultural phenomena – they just had to be present as facts belonging to Czech culture. This state of affairs opened the door to extensive borrowing from foreign sources, to the creation of cultural phenomena by analogy. The process occurred on all levels of culture, not just in philology. Czech institutions, social and political organizations, and magazines were created in analogy to primarily German culture. Czech writers entered their literature playing the part of famous figures in world literature: 'our Petrarca, our Sappho, our Homer'. This trend also implied a direct orientation towards translation 'proper'. Translation helped constitute Czech science and complete the gamut of fiction and poetry. In those days originality was primarily a characteristic of the verbal form of the text. This can easily be proved by the existence of a whole sequence of professional translations from German, such as Hýna's *Psychology* and Antonín Marek's *Logic*, published only under the names of the translators. The specific contribution of a work of literature was not thought to lie in its aesthetic value, nor was the specific purpose of a work of science thought to lie in its actual contribution to the progress of knowledge. Rather, what mattered in both cases was the mere cultivation of literary and scientific language as such. The Czech patriots did not regard language as a medium of communication. Josef Jungmann, the unofficial head of the patriotic community, the 'Sekte von böhmischen Zeloten', or the 'böhmische enragés', as a known Czech linguist and Slavist of the older generation called them (Jagić, 1885: 616, 666), formulated this shift in the function of language in a more than precise manner: 'The language is in need of cultivation, which is achieved by the cultivation of the sciences' (Jungmann, 1846: 2). Language was regarded as the aim, the acme of the national endeavour: 'In the language is our nationality' (Jungmann, 1846: 25) Jungmann has this to say about the problem of translation and originality:

The subject matter, the topic, the stuff of the mind, so to speak, is a product of the age; it does not lie in our power, and it would be absurd to care whether it is original or taken over from elsewhere. But the way in which we adopt it, the form we give it is of primary importance. (1846: 25)

Jungmann even set down three different levels for the evolution of Czech literature to pass through: 'knowledge of the language, knowledge of things, experience of the mind' (1846: 29). 'Originality' he reserved for the last phase in the evolution, projected into an uncertain future. The second level of literary development, which Jungmann obviously thought was that of his own time, was explicitly conditioned by 'the reading and translating of excellent books' (1846: 29).

   We should of course not imagine that all Czech culture of the revivalist past was produced under these absolute dictates. We ought to think more in terms of a trend, a tendency, a frame or model of cultural behaviour, within whose boundaries a dissatisfaction with the contemporary state of affairs and a real search for originality and self-expression, a resistance against the verbal, philological, 'translational' trend also found their origin. But the cultural activities which strove to create Czech culture on the basis of analogy to foreign cultural phenomena, as well as translation itself, to an even higher degree, were able to exemplify the opinions and attitudes of the Czech patriotic community. The function of revivalist translation – when the Czech literary audience was still a rather hypothetical entity, reduced to a narrow group of patriotic intellectuals – was not to mediate a foreign text, which was usually easily accessible in German. Moreover, the Czech literary language was then *in statu nascendi*, shedding German loan words in the spirit of purism, and adopting newly coined words. Very often the Czech language (*hoch Böhmisch*) was less understandable to the average Czech reader than German. This contributed to the 'shocking' strategy that Czech words in a translation were often explained by means of expressions quoted from the original. This kind of situation opened new possibilities for translation, which now acquired the character of a complex semiotic operation, a refined manipulation of foreign texts. Translation was not seen as passive submission to cultural impulses from abroad; on the contrary, it was viewed as an active, even aggressive act, an appropriation of foreign cultural values. To put it in more figurative language, translation was seen as an invasion of rival territory, an invasion undertaken with the intent of capturing rich spoils of war. In his preface to his translations from Schiller, Jan Evangelista Purkyně (Purkinjě), the Czech writer who was to become a physiologist of world renown, tried to interpret translation as an immediate reaction against the destructive impact of foreign cultures, a literal act of revenge for the damages the Slavic world had suffered in the past:

If [to the detriment of the Slavs] the Germans, Italians and Hungarians try to denationalize both our common people and our higher classes, let us use a more noble way of retaliation, taking possession of anything excellent they have created in the world of the mind. (Purkyně, 1968: 67)

The idea of the 'expropriative' function of translation lies behind a great part of the translated literature produced by the Czech Revival. It often represents the only reason why a literary work is chosen for translation. Czech literary historians have often debated why Jungmann chose to translate, of all texts, *Paradise Lost*. But they discuss the matter in terms of the present functions of translation, and fail to take into account that translation was regarded in a different manner at the beginning of the last century. They failed to notice that *Paradise Lost* really represents an amalgam of different cultures. In his epic Milton shows pagan, Christian and Jewish traditions side by side, reconciling medieval romances with biblical history and heathen myths with theological concepts of his time. All of these features, supplemented by Milton's obsession with exotic geographical names, make *Paradise Lost* into the epic of human culture, the epic of mankind as a whole. By simply transferring the poem into Czech (with the help of a number of Polish, Russian and other Slavic words), Jungmann was able to monopolize this universe for the Slavs or, in other words, to introduce the Slavs into this world side by side with the ancient Greeks, the Romans and the Indians, partners in the culture where the Czech revival tried to find its own roots. The absorption of the universal human myth by the pan-Slavic myth in the translation of *Paradise Lost* is an expression of the revivalist belief in the universal nature of Slavism, a constant element in Czech revivalist ideology and an effective antidote to the national inferiority complex.

Czech revivalist culture, with its own conception of translation and its general orientation towards translation, was therefore not condemned to silence; rather, the actual message of the time was making its way not only outside translation, but also in it and by means of it. Bowring could hardly be expected to have taken notice of this dramatic search for originality and individuality. He had not, could not have, any interest in it. On his translational expeditions he was not looking for the idyllic countries peopled by Rousseau's savages, the realms of Ossian or any nascent young cultures. Instead he expected to find new cultures, fully developed but still unknown. The Czech nation of that time was totally unable to offer him anything of the kind. All they could do was offer him a mere illusion of it, which he accepted with great enthusiasm. Bowring's 'translation as culture' (or culture-modelling translation), which seemed to have been built from the same substance as the Czech 'culture as translation', was unable to reflect the dominant 'translationality' of Czech culture the tendency to compete in the world of universal culture through analogy with foreign cultures.

The development of national cultures is marked by periods when the culture as a whole, or in part, exhibits some typological features of translation, when it takes over cultural phenomena that have originated elsewhere, and adopts them. This is a typical feature of the formative period of new national cultures, the period of 'Renaissance'. We find ample evidence of such a trend in many smaller nations of Europe, particularly in the last century. But the same phenomenon also occurs in the history of bigger nations in their periods of extensive cultural trans-orientation, as evidenced by the traditional cultures of the Orient in this and previous centuries marked by the impact of Europe.

References

Beer, Robert (ed.) (1904) *Korrespondence Johna Bowringa do Čech, Věstník Královské české společdnosti nauk, třída filozoficko-historicko-jazykozpytná*. Prague.

Bowring, John (1830) *Poetry of the Magyars, Preceded by a Sketch of the Language and Literature of Hungary and Transylvania*. London.

Čelakovský, František (1865) *Sebrané listy*. Prague.

Churchill, John and William Maginn (1830) 'The Magyars versus Dr. Bowring', *Fraser's Magazine* 2: 432–42.

Jagić, Vatroslav (ed.) (1885) *Briefwechsel zwischen Dobrowsky und Kopitar, 1808–1828*. St Petersburg.

Jungmann, Josef (1846) *Slovesnost*. Prague.

Macura, Vladimír (1983) *Znamení zrodu. České narodní obrození jako kulturní typ*. Prague: Československý spisovatel.

Purkyně, Jan Evangelista (1968) 'Básně a překlady', *Sebrané spisy* 9. Prague.

Pynsent, Robert Burton (1988) 'The Decadent Nation: The Politics of Arnošt Procházka and Jiří Karásek ze Lvovic', in *Intellectuals and the Future in the Habsburg Monarchy 1890–1914*, ed. Lászlo Péter and Robert Burton Pynsent. London: Macmillan: 63–91.

7 Linguistic Polyphony as a Problem in Translation

Elzbieta Tabakowska

Irrespective of the orientation of their proponents, linguistic models of an act of verbal communication are always seen as a triad consisting of a *sender* of the message, the *message* itself and the *receiver*. Depending on more or less explicit influences of other scholarly disciplines, the first and last elements in this neat linear arrangement are referred to as addresser and addressee, or encoder and decoder. In either case the message is conceived as being transmitted by a person speaking with one voice and willing to take full responsibility for the things he chooses to do with words. (This is true even for the proponents of speech-act theory, who have discarded the notion of an ideal speaker dear to most generative grammarians.)

Quite unpredictably, the idea of a different model came to the linguists from the adjacent, though not always readily accessible, field of literary theory. Recent work in linguistic stylistics refers more and more often to the writings of Mikhail Bakhtin, and notably to his concept of the internal dialogism of the word (Bakhtin, 1981: 279). The musical metaphor of polyphony, which Bakhtin first used to analyse Dostoevsky's novels, refers to the kind of written narrative in which the inherently dialogic character of the word as an element of natural language makes it possible for the writer to build up a chorus of voices, only one of which belongs to the writer himself. Those individual voices – or points of view, or individual languages – make up a pluralistic world in which a continual dialogue goes on, while the word itself becomes a shared property of the author, the reader, and all those who in any way participated in the creation of its history (Bakhtin, 1973; Mitosek, 1983, *passim*). In traditional linguistics, the recognition of the possibility that the word might 'belong' to people other than the actual speaker gave rise to Charles Bally's well-known distinction between personal and reported thought (*pensée personelle, pensée communiquée*). Within the general framework of generative grammar, attempts have been made to show how varying points of view temporarily adopted by speakers become reflected in their choice of particular syntactic structures (see work by Susumu Kuno and his colleagues, notably Kuno and Kaburaki, 1977, on what became known as empathy in syntax).

The ideas of Bakhtin and Bally inspired the theory of linguistic polyphony, developed by Oswald Ducrot (1980a, 1980b, 1980c, 1981, 1984, 1986). Borrowing Bakhtin's metaphor, Ducrot uses the term 'polyphony' to depict the complex nature of the entity called 'the Speaker' (or *sujet parlant*), and points out that even within a short linguistic message, such as a single sentence, the human being who produces the utterance in the technical sense of the term need not be identical with the person responsible for its wording and/or content. Examples of producers of words who are situated outside language and are thus of no interest to the linguist are the child mechanically reciting a poem and the announcer at a railway station. However, were the announcer to tell us that a train was about to arrive in tones of extreme scepticism, this expression of an attitude would add to the total meaning of the utterance. And if she were to add to her announcement the word 'perhaps!', her unwillingness to take responsibility for the statement would be explicitly marked.

But the same piece of information could also be transmitted by one prospective passenger to another, for example if one of them arrived on the platform after hearing the official announcement. The speaker need not quote the announcer's words verbatim: he might say something like 'Our train will be arriving soon', giving his message its linguistic form without, however, taking responsibility for the resulting statement. In Ducrot's terms he would then take up the role of *locuteur* (i.e. the 'author' of the message) without necessarily assuming that of *énonciateur* (i.e. the person whose point of view is being expressed): he may detach himself from it, doubt it, or positively disbelieve it. Alternatively, if he feels some confidence in the announcement, he may endorse the statement with more or less conviction, thus manifesting his solidarity with the original *énonciateur*. This possibility comes naturally as the default interpretation of what people say: unless led to believe otherwise, we assume that those who say things know, or at least believe, that what they say is true. Yet closer analysis of any type of discourse – from an impromptu verbal exchange to a fictional narrative – discloses the ubiquity of polyphony, with *locuteurs* unwilling to identify themselves with *énonciateurs*. Thus behind the single utterances are found duets, sometimes whole choirs of voices, singing in unison or discord.

In a sense it is, of course, obvious that the flow of information in verbal communication is not tantamount to the transfer of knowledge, doubt, belief or disbelief. The distinction between 'propositions' on the one hand and 'attitudes' on the other has for long occupied philosophers of language, though they find it difficult to reach consensus on what those two terms should stand for (Barwise and Perry, 1983: 177). In modern linguistics, the realization of the need to distinguish between these two aspects of verbal communication came with the development of linguistic pragmatics, initiated by scholars such as Austin, Searle and Grice. While the 'proposition' (statement, state of affairs, or 'meaning') was investigated as an abstract entity, devoid of any context that might in any way contaminate it, 'attitudes' required the introduction of the human factor: 'attitudes' belong to a definite speaker, acting within a definite situation, which is described in terms of a number of context-defining parameters. (It is precisely this human factor that separated the syntax and semantics of natural language from the pragmatics in Morris' classic tripartite system.)

Therefore, polyphony is created by individual contexts – particular complexes of spatio-temporal and sociocultural factors. It need not be explicitly marked, although it may: it is an interesting task for a linguist to look for linguistic means that speakers use to enhance it. A pragmatist looking for functional sources of grammatical constraints would be equally interested in investigating communicational aims that polyphony makes it possible to achieve. Again, the governing principle is obvious: in many cases of social interaction to accept full responsibility, in an explicit and irrevocable way, for what we say simply does not 'pay'. There are situations in which listeners might feel offended or provoked by statements that are too forward: anticipation of such reactions makes it advisable 'qu' on puisse refuser la responsabilité de leur énonciation' (Ducrot, 1980a: 5). Moreover, point-blank expressions of attitudes may be openly challenged or disputed, and the speaker's communicative strategy frequently involves dissociating himself (*bona fide* or *mala fide*) from judgements and opinions by ascribing them, in a more or less indirect way, to some other (often anonymous) party. He may also put himself in the position of a more or less accommodating *porte-parole*, expressing someone else's opinions or endorsing someone else's judgements. If he chooses one of the *mala fide* modes of communication he may only pretend endorsement, thus creating (where the pretence is to be seen through) irony or verbal humour, or (where it is not) propaganda.

All such strategies become clearly manifested in rhetorical genres of discourse – notably journalistic prose, where acts of assertion do not as a rule imply attitudes of knowledge or belief on the part of the *locuteurs*, while *énonciateurs* tend to undermine the truth of assertions which it is their job to report. For example, a recent article in *Newsweek* dealing with Colonel Gaddafi bore the heading

(1) THE ELUSIVE LIBYAN LEADER SPEAKS – SORT OF.

Linguistic polyphony has an important part to play in fictional narrative, where Bakhtin first discovered its presence. The duet inevitably following from the non-identity of author and narrator turns into a trio whenever the author resorts to the celebrated *style indirect libre*, and into a quartet when what the narrator is made to say itself becomes a composition for two voices. In his 1934 essay Bakhtin accused 'the traditional scholar' of transposing 'a symphonic (orchestrated) theme on to the piano keyboard' (Bakhtin, 1981: 263). Norman Davies, commenting on what he considered a plausible translation into Polish of one of his history books, nevertheless said that in the hands of a translator a text which was originally composed as a 'symphony in A Flat Major' may easily become 'transposed for performance by two pianos into F Sharp' (Davies, 1981).

It is a matter of course that interpretation is a prerequisite for translation. Equivalence, the term crucial to any translation theory, is still far from being adequately defined. Even so, modern translation theory generally recognizes the need for pragmatic, as well as semantic and syntactic, equivalence. Within the pragmatic category, the adequate rendering of subtle interrelations between saying things on the one hand, and knowing, believing or doubting them on the other, should certainly be considered one of the objectives of translation. A contribution from the linguist might be to provide a description of linguistic markers that enhance the polyphonic interpretation of utterances, and to point out the counterparts in the target language. Any practising translator (or teacher of language, for that matter) knows how naive it would be to believe that the task has already been accomplished by lexicographers.

From the formal point of view, linguistically marked polyphony is a dialogue deprived of the prototypical feature of turn-taking: 'une sorte de dialogue cristallisé' (Ducrot, 1980b: 49). Yet it is not tantamount either to a series of rhetorical questions (with predictable answers absent from the surface) or to a chain of answers (with hypothetical, predictable questions deleted). It has its own markers, which are often synonymous with those used to mark 'monophonic attitudes'. In translation, the attempt at full pragmatic equivalence means searching for counterparts that would not only reflect particular attitudes, but also trigger the polyphonic interpretation.

Out of the plethora of such markers, ranging from grammatical structures (e.g. impersonal verbs) to lexical items (e.g. 'hearsay particles'), I have chosen a handful of most obviously dialogic devices, employed in a sample fictional narrative – Doris Lessing's 1985 novel *The Good Terrorist* (hereafter referred to as *GT*). This novel, a glimpse into 'the world of the subsidized sub-culture of the Marxist *groupuscules* of contemporary Britain' (*Sunday Times* review), gives a portrait of Alice, the good terrorist, drawn into 'the case' by her destructively infantile lover. Although she is able to see things in their right perspective, she cannot reject the life of self-deception, and finds it impossible to go back to what is her deeply buried secret ideal: a nice, well-kept house, with flowers (her symbol of family happiness) on the sills, curtains in the windows, and a real husband coming home for dinner. She lives in a squat, where a group of people work hard to hide their middle-class origins and 'do the revolution'; she sticks to it in spite of the fact that her only true satisfaction comes from the revolutionaries' appreciation of her cooking.

Into the third-person narration merge both Alice's thought, expressed in a first-person monologue, and indirect thought explicitly attributed to her. Alice's state of 'feeling divided and confused', which is the main theme of the book, results from the clash between her two egos: the real one, and the self-imposed one. The self-deception is consistently rendered by what an analyst of the Ducrotian persuasion would classify as linguistic polyphony. While Alice herself alternatively takes the roles of two mutually opposed *énonciateurs*, the narrator or *locuteur* endorses the attitudes of the real ego. At the beginning of the story Alice's real voice is constantly suppressed by the self-imposed one; but as the plot develops the roles gradually become reversed. Thus polyphony becomes a formal device employed to show the inner transformation of the protagonist; it constitutes a part of the story, and therefore a necessary element of translation equivalence. Deceptively simple, it may escape the translator's attention entirely; and if noticed, it may prove difficult to render.

Early in the story she catches herself worrying about the risks being run by her boy-friend, and tells herself that

(2) It was not that she wanted him safe, but that she wanted things done right. (*GT*: 79)

Further on, the anti-revolutionary act of buying a new boiler for the dilapidated squat is justified with

(3) Not that Alice cared about warmth, not after four years in her mother's house. (*GT*: 155)

Unlike the more commonly used verbal negation, outside the field of formal logic, the sentence negation exemplified in (2) and (3) has a clearly polemical character. The writer translating this passage into Polish is faced with two alternatives, depending on whether he interprets 'the other voice' as an anticipated reproach from Alice's fellow revolutionaries, or as the inner voice of her alter ego: (a) the conditional *nie żeby* + past-tense verb; or (b) the affirmative *nieprawda, że* + present-tense verb:

(2)a Nie żeby chciała . . .
(2)b Nieprawda, że chce . . .
(3)a Nie żeby jej zależało . . .
(3)b Nieprawda, że jej zależy . . .

(See the discussion of *il est faux que* in Ducrot 1980c: 94, and the definition of the act of denial in Lyons, 1977: 770 ff.)

Alice's constant longing for approval and appreciation – especially from the powerful and mysterious Comrade Andrew – is signalled by the double negation and the particle·'surely' in

(4) He had his eyes intent on her. . . . It was a detached, cold scrutiny. Not hostile, not unfriendly, surely? (*GT*: 116)

Ignoring bilingual dictionary information, the translator will choose as the pragmatic equivalent of 'surely' the 'persuasive particle' *przecież*: the context suggests that Alice tries to force herself to believe what the voice of common sense tells her to reject:

(4)a Ale przecież nie wrogie, nie nieprzyjazne?

An exceptional act of mere honesty (just for once, the notorious Jasper decides to give Alice her share of the dole) is interpreted as a proof of love:

(5) He did love her. He did. (*GT*: 103)

The stressed 'emphatic *do*' expresses an act of confirmation, by the superimposed self, of what the other Alice has been desperately trying to believe. Because of the lack of a parallel syntactic device, Polish requires the use of a more explicitly dialogic expression, e.g. *więc jednak* (literally 'so after all'):

(5) a Więc jednak ją kocha. Kocha.

As the story progresses, Alice the revolutionary has more and more often to admit what the real Alice tells her – for instance, that Jasper is not being taken seriously by anyone:

(6) Many people were busy with conversations. These were not, in fact, about the CCU, or indeed, about anything that Jasper had said; his opening speech was hardly mentioned. (*GT*: 221–2)

As before, the context demands the polyphonic interpretation of the two hedges (in fact' and 'indeed'); in Polish, it might be additionally enhanced by supplementing the lexical equivalents with the particle *to*, which in a truly dialogical discourse performs the function of a 'pointer', pointing back to an earlier turn:

(6)a . . . właściwie to nie dotyczyła ona CCU, ani prawdę mówiąc . . .

Towards the end of the novel illusions die, and the voice of the real

Alice takes over:

(7) Yes, he had been nice to make up for it. But he had not told her! He had never before so betrayed her. (*GT*: 247)

The pragmatic equivalent of the dialogic 'Yes' in (7), i.e. *owszem* (cf. French *d'accord*), is described by Polish linguists as one of the 'appositions ... which function as plausible answers to questions' (Grochowski, 1986: 12):

(7) a Owszem, był 'miły', żeby jej to wynagrodzić. Ale ...

When Alice finally decides to move out, she openly rejects what her revolutionary ego politely whispers in her ear:

(8) It was all enough. It was too much. If Jasper wanted her, he would have to come and find her.

And no, she would not be leaving an address. (*GT*: 267)

Again, rather than simple negation, translation equivalence requires an expression of strong denial, for example *wykluczone* (literally 'out of the question'):

(8) a ... Wyukluczone, nie zostawi adresu.

Like polyphony itself, translation is discourse-oriented. The linguistic minutiae that enhance it may go unnoticed by a hasty interpreter. The melody remains, but a symphony written in A Flat Major becomes transposed into F Sharp for performance by two pianos.

References

Bakhtin, M. (1973) 'Slowo w poezji i slowo w prozie', trans. Janina Walicka, *Litratura na Swiecie* 6(26): 3–47.

Bakhtin, M. (1981) *The Dialogic Imagination*, trans. and ed. Michael Holquist. Austin, TX: University of Texas Press.

Barwise, J. and John Perry (1983) *Situations and Attitudes*. Cambridge, MA: MIT Press.

Davies, N. (1981) *God's Playground: The History of Poland*, 2 vols. Oxford, Clarendon Press.

Ducrot, O. (1980a) *Dire et ne pas dire. Principes de semantique linguistique.* Paris: Collection Savoir.

Ducrot, O. (1980b) *Les mots du discours.* Paris: Les Editions de Minuit.

Ducrot, O. (1980c) *Les échelles argumentatives.* Paris: Les Editions de Minuit.

Ducrot, O. (1981) 'L'Argumentation par authorité', in *L'Argumentation*. Lyon: Presses Universitaires.

Ducrot, O. (1984) *Le dire et le dit.* Paris: Les Editions de Minuit.

Ducrot, O. (1986) 'Charles Bally et la pragmatique', *Cahiers Ferdinand de Saussure* 40: 13–37.

Grochowski, M. (1986) *Polskie partykuly. Skladnia, semantyka, leksykografia.* Wroclaw: Ossolineum.

Kuno, S. and Etsuko Kaburaki (1977) 'Empathy and Syntax', *Linguistic Inquiry* 8 (4): 627–72.

Lyons, J. (1977) *Semantics*, Vol. II. Cambridge: Cambridge University Press.

Mitosek, Z. (1983) *Teorie badan literackich.* Warszawa: PWN.

8 Linguistic Transcoding or Cultural Transfer? A Critique of Translation Theory in Germany

Mary Snell-Hornby

Since the days of Martin Luther, Germany has played a pioneering role in both the theory and practice of translation, and yet in English writings on translation theory this rich fund of scholarship and experience is rarely more than briefly mentioned. Evidently even translation scholars have problems with language barriers. In recent years there has been a ferment of new ideas on translation in the German-speaking countries, many of them hotly debated in countless publications, but in the English-speaking world the household names of German translation theory remain virtually unknown. As an attempt to counteract the deficit, this paper presents an overview of the two main streams in translation theory that have developed in Germany since the war: the linguistically oriented *Übersetzungswissenschaft* as represented in particular by the theorists of the Leipzig School, along with Wolfram Wilss and Werner Koller, and the culturally oriented approach of scholars such as Hans J. Vermeer. By way of conclusion, an alternative concept will be outlined for an integrated approach to translation, where possible linking the German theories to what has developed in English as translation studies, and in particular linking the field of literary translation theory to relevant approaches in linguistics.

For 2,000 years translation theory (some call it 'traditional', others now dismiss it as 'pre-scientific') was primarily concerned with outstanding works of art. The focus was therefore on literary translation, and at the centre of the debate was that age-old dichotomy of word and sense, of 'faithful' versus 'free' translation. The picture changed suddenly after the Second World War, along with the euphoria that hailed machine translation in the early 1950s, when there was a call for scientific rigour within the field of translation, to replace what was felt to be hazy speculation. This gave rise to the 'science of translating' as understood by Nida (1964) and to the school of *Übersetzungswissens- chaft* that developed in Germany. This branch of translation studies was for a long time clearly defined as a sub-discipline of applied linguistics, whose aims and methods were unquestioningly adopted. Just as linguistics aims at making the study of language strictly scientific, *Übersetzungswissenschaft*, at least in the early days, aimed at making the study of translation rigorously scientific and watertight, and like linguistics, it adopted views and methods of the exact sciences, in particular mathematics and formal logic. Basically, trans- lation was viewed as linguistic transcoding, as emerges clearly from Koller's definition of translation from a book published in 1972:[1] Linguistically, he maintains, translation can be described as transcod- ing or substitution, whereby Elements a_1, a_2, a_3 of the inventory of linguistic signs L_1 are replaced by Elements b_1, b_2, b_3 of the inventory of linguistic signs L_2. (1972: 69–70)

In this view, language is seen as a code relating to a system of universals, and the differing elements of two languages are linked by a common interlingual *tertium comparationis* by virtue of which they can be described as 'equivalent'.

The Illusion of Equivalence

The concept of equivalence was basic to any linguistically oriented translation theory, whether the scholars concerned wrote in English (Catford, 1965; Nida and Taber, 1969) or German (Kade, 1968; Reiss, 1971; Wilss, 1977). It is however a highly controversial con- cept, and despite a heated debate of over twenty years, it was never satisfactorily defined in its relevance to translation. Elsewhere I have shown (Snell-Hornby, 1986b; 13–16, 1988: 13–22) that the English term 'equivalence' and the German term *Äquivalenz* are not even, in the strictly scientific sense, themselves equivalent. This may·be why, for the pragmatic Anglo-Saxon mind, the German debate on the topic seems so strangely dogmatic and remote from reality: whereas in English the adjective 'equivalent' has been used since 1460 in its commonsense, rather fuzzy everyday sense of 'virtually the same thing', 'of similar significance', the concept of *Äquivalenz* was taken over into German *Übersetzungswissenschaft* as a strictly scientific term from either mathematics or formal logic (or both) during the early era of machine translation (Wilss, 1977), hence from the outset the element of reversibility was salient.[2]

Not surprisingly, in this approach the concept of *Äquivalenz* proved more suitable at the level of the individual word than at the level of the text, and it was best applied in the systemic area of contrastive linguistics as against the act of translating. In other words, the term *Äquivalenz* had its best results in the field of contrastive lexicology. A great deal of work was done on the topic in Leipzig (see for example Jäger and Neubert, 1982); particularly well known are the four equivalence types presented by Otto Kade (1968). These are (1) *total* equivalence as found in completely identical terms and standardized terminology; (2) *facultative* equivalence (one-to-many), as exemplified in German *Spannung* against English voltage, tension, suspense, stress, pressure; (3) *approximative* equivalence (one-to-part-of-one) as in German *Himmel* compared with English heaven/sky; and (4) *nil*-equivalence as in culture-bound items like wicket and haggis. At this stage it was still assumed that the language system could be equated with the concrete realization in a text, whereby the system provided 'potential equivalents' from which the translator selected the 'optimal' equivalent for the case in question. Gradually it was realized however that translation involves more than merely a loose sequence of individual words, and the concept of the 'translation unit' was developed as a basis for a scientific approach to translation: at first this was identified as the phrase or idiom between the levels of word and sentence, but gradually the view gained ground that the only possible basis for comparison in translation was the complete text itself. These various positions are co-ordinated in the pioneer study by Katharina Reiss (1971), which demands equivalence both at the level of the text and between individual translation units (1971: 11–12). Reiss' main contribution to translation theory in this study however lies in the criteria she offers for translation critique, which depend basically – not on the lexical item as with Kade – on the global *text-type* of the work concerned. Such text-types are defined as *informative* (e.g. a scientific report), *expressive* (e.g. a lyric poem) and *conative* (e.g. an advertisement).[3]

The limited scope of this essay does not permit even a superficial discussion of the finer points and problems arising from either the equivalence debate or from Katharina Reiss' text-types (for which reference is made to Snell-Hornby, 1988); what has emerged from the above outline however is the crucial shift of focus from the isolated lexical item in a language system to the differentiated handling of texts in the act of translation. This has been taken very much further in the more recent approaches to translation studies.

Recent Translation Theories

What is dominant in the series of new approaches recently presented in Germany (in particular Hönig and Kussmaul, 1982; Reiss and Vermeer, 1984; Holz-Mänttäri, 1984; see also the collection of essays in Snell-Hornby, 1986a) is the orientation towards *cultural* rather than linguistic transfer; secondly, they view translation not as a process of transcoding but as an *act* of *communication*; thirdly, they are all oriented towards the *function* of the *target text* (prospective translation) rather than prescriptions of the source text (retrospective translation); fourthly, they view the text as an *integral part of the world* and not as an isolated specimen of language. These basic similarities are so striking that it is not exaggerated to talk of a new orientation in translation theory.

The major theoretical contribution in this approach has been made by Hans J. Vermeer, whose *Skopostheorie*, based on the function of the translated text (Gk. *skopos* = aim, target), is presented in Reiss and Vermeer (1984).

Vermeer has for many years vehemently opposed the view that translation is simply a matter of language: for him translation is primarily a crosscultural transfer (see Vermeer, 1986), and in his view the translator should be bicultural, if not multicultural, which naturally involves a command of various languages, as language is an intrinsic part of culture. Secondly, Vermeer sees translation essentially as a form of action, a 'Sondersorte von Handeln' (1986: 36), in other words, it could be described as a 'crosscultural event' (cf. Snell-Hornby, 1987). This applies to language-pairs that are culturally closely related (like English and German) as well as to language-pairs with only distant cultural connections (such as Finnish and Chinese): the difference is one of degree and not of kind. Vermeer describes his concept of translation as follows:

Translation is not the transcoding of words or sentences from one language to another, but a complex form of action, whereby someone provides information on a text (source language material) in a new situation and under changed functional, cultural and linguistic conditions, preserving formal aspects as closely as possible. (1986: 33)

But the dominating feature of Vermeer's approach is the function of the target text, which may well differ from the original function of the source text. In this context Vermeer has introduced the two terms *Funktionskonstanz* (unchanged function) and *Funktionsveränderung* (changed function, whereby the text is adapted to meet specified needs in the target culture). A striking example is the case of advertising texts: the function of the text is preserved if the translation is likewise to be an advertisement addressed to potential customers with the intention of selling the product. It is changed if, for example, the text is used for information purposes, as on marketing conventions and strategies in the source culture. This observation implies something very important, which was largely ignored in both the traditional and the linguistic approach to translation: 'the' translation *per se* does not exist, and neither does the 'perfect translation'. A translation is directly dependent on its prescribed function, which must be made clear from the start. For Vermeer translation is always relative to the given situation, and thus his approach is essentially *dynamic*. He himself describes it as follows:

As we cannot say that a given text *is* a pragmatic text, *is* a piece of propaganda, but only that it *is intended* to be one, is understood, translated or interpreted as such, we have to choose a more dynamic wording and say that the decision depends on the aim of the translation. (Reiss and Vermeer, 1984: 29)

A very similar approach to translation, but with a more linguistic bias, is presented in the very appealing book *Strategie der Übersetzung* by Hans G. Hönig and Paul Kussmaul (1982). This is actually intended as a textbook for students in the translator-training institutes, and the fact that it has a rich fund of illustrative examples and is written in a lively style enhances rather than detracts from its theoretical worth. Hönig and Kussmaul's starting point is the conception of the text as what they call 'the verbalized part of a socio-culture' (1982: 58): the text is embedded in a given situation, which is itself conditioned by its sociocultural background. The translation is then dependent on its function as a text 'implanted' in the target culture. The basic criterion for assessing the quality of a translation is called the 'necessary grade of differentiation', which represents 'the point of intersection between target text function and socio-cultural determinants' (1982: 53). To illustrate this they quote two sentences, each naming a famous British public school:

In Parliament he fought for equality, but *he sent his son to Winchester.*

When his father died *his mother couldn't afford to send him to Eton any more.*

They then quote two extreme types of German translation:

. . . seinen eigenen Sohn schickte er auf die Schule in Winchester.

. . . konnte es sich seine Mutter nicht mehr leisten, ihn nach Eton zu schicken, jene teure englische Privatschule, aus deren Absolventen auch heute noch ein Grossteil des politischen und wirtschaftlichen Führungsnachwuchses hervorgeht. (1982: 58)

The first translation is under-differentiated: the mere name 'Winchester' does not carry the same meaning for a German reader as for an English one. The second translation is over-differentiated: however correct the information on British public schools may be, it is superfluous to the text concerned.[4] In the first of the two English sentences, it is the double-faced hypocrisy of the father (hence the exclusive, elitist character of public schools) that is stressed, while the second focuses on an impoverished widowed mother (and the expensive school fees). As the necessary grade of differentiation for the texts in question, the authors therefore suggest:

Im Parlament kämpfte er für die Chancengleichheit, aber seinen eigenen Sohn schickte er auf *eine der englischen Eliteschulen.*

Als sein Vater starb, konnte seine Mutter es sich nicht mehr leisten, ihn auf *eine der teuren Privatschulen* zu schicken.

An integrated approach

The two basic approaches to translation theory outlined here both focus on specialized or general language, and on pragmatic rather than literary texts, and they are taught in training institutes which do not cater for literary translators. Literary translation, which in the last few years has attracted a good deal of attention in Germany, is considered to be part of comparative literature and is still the domain of the literature departments.[5] In this respect it corresponds to what in English is called translation studies (as represented by scholars from the Low Countries, Israel, Great Britain, Canada and the USA). It is a sad fact that the linguistic and literary approaches to translation have up to now been mutually exclusive. In the linguistically oriented *Übersetzungswissenschaft* literary translation was explicitly ruled out as being 'deviant', the 'free play with creative and expressive elements in language' (Wilss, 1977: 181) and hence beyond all scientific objectivity. Conversely, scholars in literary translation reject the linguistic approach as useless for their purposes (Hermans, 1985: 10).

The culturally oriented approach to translation theory has some potential for bridging the gap, and indeed it implicitly embraces all kinds of translation. Furthermore, its orientation towards the target text as part of the target culture coincides exactly with the major tenet of literary translation studies as expounded in Hermans (1985). In fact however, it seems less applicable to literary translation than it is to specialized or general language texts: firstly, in a literary work of art, the source text has a different status than in an advertisement or legal contract; secondly, in the case of a literary text the factors of situation and function are infinitely more complex than in pragmatic texts; and thirdly, the factor of style, which in literary translation is so important, has in non-literary translation theory barely been considered. This does not mean that Vermeer's cultural approach is irrelevant to literary translation – but it does mean that a number of points need rethinking.

I would maintain that an integrated approach to translation is not only possible, but that it is even essential if translation studies is to establish itself as an independent discipline, as against two separate sub-disciplines of the two different subject areas applied linguistics and literary criticism. In a recent study with the title *Translation Studies – An Integrated Approach* (Snell-Hornby, 1988) I have tried to show that there are indeed linguistic concepts and methods which – given an undogmatic and flexible interpretation – can be used for varying types of text from a story by Dylan Thomas to a conference circular or public road sign. Especially productive for translation are some concepts from text linguistics, prototype semantics, contrastive grammar and the speech-act theory.

The rigorously linguistic conception of translation as mere substitution or transcoding has now been largely abandoned, even for special language translation, whereas the potential in the culturally oriented approach has yet to be exploited. Beyond this general conclusion which can be drawn from our brief outline of modern German translation theory, there are however at least two salient points that have emerged from the discussion which may prove vital for the discipline of the future. Firstly, whether or not one may agree with the individual theories, the fact remains that they have provided basic concepts and terminology, as well as an urgently needed frame of reference, without which no scholarly discipline can develop. Secondly, while in Germany much has been done to institutionalize the varying sub-fields of translation studies, no significant attempt has been made to bring them together. A bridge across the gulf has yet to be built, so that, when two translation scholars from different countries and different backgrounds talk about translation, they may have some common ground.

Notes

1. In order for this paper to fulfil its intended function of overcoming the language barrier, German quotations are given in literal English translation, followed by the bibliographical reference.
2. Note that this also applies to the English technical term *equivalence*, as in mathematics, also as a linguistic term in transformational grammar.
3. This is based on Bühler's theory of text functions (1934). Reiss adds a fourth text-type, the *audio-medial*, to refer to the language of theatre, film, etc.
4. In literal translation: '. . . that expensive English public school which even today produces many of the future leaders in politics and management'.
5. This is the case both in the few courses offered in literary translation and in the research projects (c.f. the works of the Göttingen group of translation studies scholars).

References

Bühler, Karl (1934) *Sprachtheorie. Die Darstellungsfunktion der Sprache.* Stuttgart: Fischer.
Catford, John C. (1965) *A Linguistic Theory of Translation.* London: Oxford University Press.

Hermans, Theo (ed.) (1985) *The Manipulation of Literature. Studies in Literary Translation.* London: Croom 'Helm.

Holz-Mänttäri, Justa (1984) *Translatorisches Handeln. Theorie und Methode.* Helsinki: Suomalainen Tiedeakatemia.

Hönig, Hans G. and Paul Kussmaul (1982) *Strategie der Übersetzung. Ein Lehr- und Arbeitsbuch.* Tübingen: Narr.

Jäger, Gert and Albrecht Neubert (eds) (1982) *Äquivalenz bei der Translation.* Leipzig: Enzyklopädie.

Kade, Otto (1968) *Zufall und Gesetzmässigkeit in der Übersetzung.* Leipzig: Enzyklopädie.

Koller, Werner (1972) *Grundprobleme der Übersetzungstheorie. Unter besonderer Berücksichtigung schwedisch-deutscher Übersetzungsfälle.* Berne: Francke.

Nida, Eugene A. (1964) *Toward a Science of Translating. With Special Reference to Principles and Procedures Involved in Bible Translating.* Leiden: Brill.

Nida, Eugene A. and Charles R. Taber (1969) *The Theory and Practice of Translation.* Leiden: Brill.

Reiss, Katharina (1971) *Möglichkeiten und Grenzen der Übersetzungskritik. Kategorien und Kriterien für eine sachgerechte Beurteilung von Übersetzungen.* Munich: Hueber.

Reiss, Katharina and Hans J. Vermeer (1984) *Grundlegung einer allgemeinen Translationstheorie.* Tübingen: Niemeyer.

Snell-Hornby, Mary (ed.) (1986a) *Übersetzungswissenschaft – Eine Neuorientierung. Zur Integrierung von Theorie und Praxis.* Tübingen: Francke.

Snell-Hornby, Mary (1986b) 'Übersetzen, Sprache, Kultur', in Snell-Hornby (1986a): 9–29.

Snell-Hornby, Mary (1987) 'Translation as a Cross-cultural Event: *Midnight's Children – Mitternachtskinder*', *Indian Journal of Applied Linguistics*, 2: 91–105.

Snell-Hornby, Mary (1988) *Translation Studies – An Integrated Approach.* Amsterdam: Benjamins.

Vermeer, Hans J. (1986) 'Übersetzen als kultureller Transfer', in Snell-Hornby (1986a): 30–53.

Wilss, Wolfram (1977) *Übersetzungswissenschaft. Probleme und Methoden.* Stuttgart: Klett.

9 Theorizing Feminist Discourse/Translation

Barbara Godard

The only complete reading is the one which transforms the book into a simultaneous network of reciprocal relationships. (Derrida, 1978: 24.)

Questions of language and gender, women's troubling relationship with language, have emerged as a central preoccupation of feminist theory and in the translation of women writers.[1] Increasingly, translations of texts by French feminist theorists with their playful disruptions of the dominant discourse have posed great challenges to the translator. To raise the issue of their translation in the framework of language, gender and ideology is to ask about the relationship between the theories of discourse advanced in these texts and the theories of translation which have produced the English version. Are the texts grounded in theories of equivalency (sameness), or does the meaning of the translation come from its redistributive function, as transformation? Do the translations seek to hide the work of translation and appear as naturalized in the English language, or do they function as texts, as writing, and foreground their work upon meaning?

Both theoreticians of women's discourse and of feminist translation ground their reflection in issues of identity and difference, otherness being framed linguistically in terms of gender as well as of nationality. Madeleine Gagnon develops parallels between the colonized position of Quebec and the linguistic alienation of women. Positing the existence of two language worlds, those of men and women, she advocates that women use the language of the dominant to persuade and to transform it. Masquerade: 'M'approprier cette langue qui pourtant est mienne mais étrange. La disposer à ma guise et je ne *traduis* pas. (Gagnon, 1977: 69).

Mais nous, nous avons la parole, nous avons multiplicités de paroles; celle des discours mâles qui peuvent encore servir: prenons-là [*sic*], nettoyons-la de toutes ses aliénations; reconnaissons ses marques phalliques et ajoutons le double du sexe qui manque; faisons notre marque; puis, nous avons la nôtre, notre parole, à inventer, à mesure que l'éveil de notre sexe se poursuit: car s'il fut refoulé par les mâles, il fut par nous, d'une certaine façon, camouflé. (1977: 82)

This doubled language, male discourse re-marked by the multiplicity of women's speech, will transform scientific discourse and its poetics of transparence. As an emancipatory practice, feminist discourse is a political discourse directed towards the construction of new meanings and is focused on subjects creating themselves in/by language. (Elshtain, 1982: 617). It seeks to expose ideological modes of perception through an expansion of messages in which individual and collective experience originate from a critical stance against the social contexts of patriarchy and its language. In this, feminist texts generate a theory of the text as critical transformation.

The possibility of future feminist intervention requires an ironic manipulation of the semiotics of performance and production. From Suzanne Lamy, we learn about the way feminist discourse works upon the dominant discourse in a complex and ambiguous movement between discourses. Women's discourse is double;[2] it is the echo of the self and the other, a movement into alterity. 'Cette parole toute de souplesse et de mouvements secrets vire en un discours en écho de soi-même et de l'autre.' (Lamy, 1979: 46).[3] Mobility is evident in the way women's discourse circulates from speech to writing, operating *in between*, intervening 'Comment cerner cet *entre* qui disjoint parole et écriture? Comme mode d'intervention, la parole des femmes garde intact ses devoirs: les tâches à accomplir sont immenses" (p. 54). Speech, as gossip, as private communication among women, is non-sense (p. 33): it works upon language anarchically, shattering everything ('Activité anarchique, le bavardage que j'aime – celui qui *me travaille* – fait voler en éclats tout ce qui tente de se coller à lui'). But from this rupture may come meaning of a new order, not that of 'cohérence et d'unification' but of 'mouvance et pluralité' (p. 21). In the to and fro movement, writing is rupture and plurality. Anchored in the collectivity of women, with an implicit feminist agenda, and characterized by a theoretical discourse which problematizes language, women's writing gives rise to: 'des textes qui rendent compte d'une différenciation qui peut se manifester de façon polymorphe, sous les aspects de l'éclatement, de la pluralité, de la rupture, de l'absence de structure close . . .' (p. 64).

This polymorphic quality makes of feminist discourse an 'écriture à deux' (p. 39), 'un dialogue au sens plein du terme' (p. 45). Dialogic, the-one-within-the-other in the Bakhtinian sense of the polyphonic text, feminist discourse works to subvert the monologism of the dominant discourse.

Translation, in its figurative meanings of transcoding and transformation, is a topos in feminist discourse used by women writers to evoke the difficulty of breaking out of silence in order to communicate new insights into women's experiences and their relation to language. Confronted with a plurality of discourses, the mixture of levels of language within one national culture or heteroglossia, wherein their language is marginal with respect to the dominant discourse, women writers figure this metaphorically in terms of polyglossia or the co-presence of several 'foreign' languages. Where the political and social dimensions of the languages are prominent, as in the case of feminism, the confrontational encounter of languages becomes explicit. Women writers experience the conflict of heteroglossia in a specific way as a deterrent to participation in a national tradition. The traces of this conflict have been defined as a translation effect, or 'l'épreuve de létranger'. To Antoine Berman, the dis/placement in language effected by a foreigner such as Conrad or Beckett writing in a second language is like that of the literary work in a foreign language translated into English or French, producing an estrangement effect or defamiliarization, the *work* of translation. (Berman, 1984: 18n.). Although framed as a transfer from one language to another, feminist discourse involves the transfer of a cultural reality into a new context as an operation in which literary traditions are variously challenged in the encounter of differing modes of textualization.

Everywhere women are writing their way into subjective agency, dis/placing themselves. There is a widespread feeling that it has been necessary to invent a new language to discuss what has been taboo. 'Inédit', unwritten, is a recurrent term in Nicole Brossard's writing to describe her work expressing such 'unknown' experiences of women, unknown, that is, within the dominant discourse which has positioned women as non-sense. The complex process of inscribing this unrecorded emotion is conveyed in her poem sequence, *L'Aviva* in terms of a double movement of translation where the emotion is first voiced and heard, then 'translated' and acted upon in sextual pleasure.[4] In a second moment, this emotion of 'l'aviva' is translated phonetically: 'l'en suite traduite'.[5] The epigraph to this sequence of poems announces that 'l'émotion est un signe/une réplique attentive au sens.' The poems unfold in tandem: emotion is located and voiced, then translated by the poet into text through a process of sound association and play on words which effect a transformation in the material signifier like the reverberations and mimicry of the echo. ('La peau de décrire un instant' becomes 'l'eau qui décrit car c'est lent.')

The dialogic moment of translation is at the centre of *Le désert mauve*, a fiction in which Brossard is translating herself, underlining the double activity of women's writing as reading/writing, as the re/reading of the already-written followed by the divining/writing of the unrecorded.[6] The poetics of transparence and ethics of wholeness of writing oneself into existence through writing directly one's own experience, is called into question through an examination and displacement of their reading effects. In its place is a poetics of identity that engages with the 'other woman'. 'Transformance', it might well be called, to emphasize the work of translation, the focus on the process of constructing meaning in the activity of transformation, a mode of performance. This is to evoke the sound poem *Trance(dance)form* performed by Penny Kemp. (Kemp, n.d.) To adopt this term is to underline the interweaving of feminist writing and feminist translation for 'Transformance' is also the collective title for the re/writing (translation) project in which Nicole Brossard has been involved with Daphne Marlatt (Marlatt and Brossard, 1985, 1986). Brossard's activities of transformance stand as a model for feminist discourse/translation in its actions of re/reading and re/writing, its dialogism.

Feminist discourse is translation in two ways: as notation of 'gestural' and other codes from what has been hitherto 'unheard of', a muted discourse (Irigaray, 1985: 134, 132), and as repetition and consequent displacement of the dominant discourse. Both set out to 'destroy the discursive mechanism' by assuming the feminine role deliberately, in an act of 'mimicry', which is to convert a form of subordination into an affirmation and to challenge an order resting on sexual indifference. The effects of this 'playful repetition' make visible what has been concealed, that is the operation of the feminine in language and the fact that women are good 'mimics' because they are never reabsorbed in this function (p. 76). In this logic of 'supplementarity', 'an *other* writing necessarily entails an *other* economy of meaning' (p. 131). Feminist discourse works upon language, upon the dominant discourse, in a radical interrogation of meaning. '[The language work's] function would thus be to cast phallogocentrism loose from its moorings in order to return the masculine to its own language, leaving open the possibility of a different language. Which means that the masculine would no longer be "everything" '(p. 80).

Translation, in this theory of feminist discourse, is production, not reproduction, the *mimesis* which is 'in the realm of music' (p. 131) and which, by an 'effect of playful repetition' – 'women also remain elsewhere' (p. 76) – makes visible the place of women's exploitation by discourse. Pretensions to the production of a singular truth and meaning are suspended. This theory focuses on feminist discourse in its transtextual or hypertextual relations, as palimpsest working on problematic notions of identity, dependency and equivalence.[7] It is mimicry, repetition which redoubles as it crosses back and forth through the mirror, a logic of disruptive excess in which nothing is ever posited that is not also reversed. Linear meaning is no longer possible in a situation caught up in the supplementarity of this reversal (p. 80). In this, feminist discourse presents transformation as performance as a model for translation. Transformation of the text is conceived within the axioms of topology. However, this is at odds with the long dominant theory of translation as equivalence grounded in a poetics of transparence.

Translation theory and practice have varied over the centuries. Each age has its own theory. Currently dominant is a theory of translation as equivalence which is grounded in a poetics of transparency. It maintains that a message may be transposed from one language to another so that the meaning of the message is preserved and there is an identity of content in the two texts: 'La traduction consiste à produire dans la langue d'arrivée *l'équivalent naturel* le plus proche du message de la langue du départ, d'abord quant à la signification, puis quant au style' (Mounin, 1963: xii; my emphasis). There is perceived to be no opposition between signifier and signified, but an isomorphism, a complete parallelism of the content and expression, of meaning and sound (p. 97). Such a translation is characterized by the way in which certain cultural traces and also certain self-reflexive elements are eliminated from the text so that the translated text is deprived of its foundation in events. The elimination of self-reflexive elements results in the suppression of signs of the author-function but also in those of the translator-function since her manipulative work on these elements is rendered invisible in the resulting conflation of the two texts. In this way are effaced the translator's dual activities of reading and (re)writing. The translator is understood to be a servant, an invisible hand mechanically turning the words of one language into another. The translation is considered to be a copy and not a creative utterance. In the twentieth century, this theory of translation has served to encourage experiments in machine translation.

What such a theory of translation based on equivalency ignores is the extreme difficulty in translating meaning because of the import-ance of co-textual (formal) and contextual relationships (Catford, 1965: 36). Recent theories of translation address these relationships and move in a new direction to emphasize the work of the translator as decoder and re-encoder. Translation is not merely a transcoding operation: the English 'yes' is not the same as the French 'oui' because there is also the French 'si'. Translators each have their favourite list of context-bound objects used to illustrate the fact that language is not transparent. Each language classifies and organizes the world and the translator creatively intervenes in such instances.

Contemporary theories of translation stress that equivalence in translation should not be approached as a search for sameness. It is perceived as a dialectic between signs and structures within and surrounding source language and target language texts (Bassnett-

McGuire, 1980: 29). Equivalence is located between the coding-decoding operations of two text *systems* rather than between the contents or words of two messages. As Bassnett/McGuire frames this: Author–Text–Receiver = Translator–Text–Receiver (p. 38). Like the author, the translator is the producer of an utterance. Bassnett-McGuire also invites us to consider the relationships between the two communicative systems in terms of intertextuality (1980: 79).

While intertextuality is a new concept in translation theory, such theories of the text as productivity and permutation (as intertextuality) have gained currency in semiotic approaches to literary theory, where a shift in focus from author to text and then to reader and the act of enunciation has already occurred. In translation theory, pragmatics understands the translator to be an active reader first before becoming a writer: s/he is both receiver and sender of the utterance, the end and the beginning of two separate but linked chains of communication. The result, according to Octavio Paz, is 'translations of translations of translations. . . . Every text is unique and at the same time it is the translation of another text. . . . Every translation, up to a certain point, is an invention and as such it constitutes a unique text' (Bassnett-McGuire, 1980: 38). 'The translation of a text structured like a text, functioning like a text, it is writing of a reading/writing, the historical adventure of a subject. It is not transparent with respect to the original' but as 'transformation' works upon the original to decentre it (Meschonnic, 1973: 307; my translation). Here, translation theory rejoins feminist textual theory in emphasizing the polyphony of the translated text in that it foregrounds the self-reflexive elements of the translator's/rewriter's discourse and flaunts its work, its textuality.

Translation is one among many ways of rewriting within literary systems pushing them in a certain direction through canonizations.[8] New theoretical models derived from other systems of rewriting are needed to describe more precisely this paradigm of translation as a manipulation of texts whose meaning is derived from their transformation. Both quotation and parody concern themselves with interdiscursive repetition, repetition considered to be a thing in itself, a fact of language. Both address themselves to the ambiguities of repetition, to the fact that nothing is more refutable than the equivalence of two propositions. On the one hand is the observation that things are repeated, on the other the realization that repetition is a fact of language from which meaning is produced, as in the case of the refrain or rhyme. The semantic confusions which disturb the order of words in quotation between mention and use, between meaning and denotation, involve a distinction between two levels of language, a language-object and a metalanguage. The effect of this disturbance of the levels of language is to substitute for the meaning of the word, the meaning of the repetition of the word (Compagnon, 1979: 86). The value of repetition is a supplement of meaning. The repetition of the words of others, quotation can only be the simulacra-phantasm in the Platonic system of *mimesis*, the impure form and not the icon-copy, or the pure form, a resemblance and not the truth (1979: 125). As such it is para-doxal, both like and unlike the doxa.

Parody too is both like and unlike, a singalong and a countersong, a re- or trans-contextualizing of previous works of art (Hutcheon, 1985: 11). Like quotation and other modes of repetition, parody is a *mise-en-abyme*, a 'mirroring' of the origins of the process of realistic figuration and consequently has a meta-fictional function (Payant, 1980: 29). Like translation, parody consists of two text-worlds, those of parodist and target, received by the reader at another time and place and based on two connected models of communication. The source work is decoded by the parodist as reader and then encoded again in a changed form for another decoder, the reader, who will have pre-viously read and decoded the source work (Rose, 1979: 26). Parody depends on the reader's 'sideward glance' (Bakhtin, 1984: 199) of recognition to activate the supplement. This lays bare the fictiveness of fiction and foregrounds its devices, so enabling them to be refunc-tioned for new purposes. There is an emphasis on transformation, on the role of the artist/translator as active reader and writer, and hence on the complex act of enunciation within this communication system. Even though its hypertext may be illusory, invisible behind the reproduction, translation may be categorized as 'forgerie', and de-fined as 'imitation sur le régime sérieux' (Genette, 1982: 37). As neutral ethos (Hutcheon, 1981: 149), parody becomes a definition for all mimesis, that is for any form of redoubling. In light of this re-writing, the concept of translation is enlarged to include imitation, adaptation, quotation, pastiche, parody – all different modes of re-writing: in short, all forms of interpenetration of works and discourses.

When translation is concerned not only with the relationship between two languages but between two text systems, literary transla-tion becomes a text in its own right so that the traditional boundary set up to separate original works from their translations collapses. 'La distinction traditionelle entre texte et traduction,' writes Meschonnic, 'apparaît comme une catégorie idéaliste. Elle est ici annulée' (1973: 365). As a corollary, there is a reassessment of the status of the source text overvalued in theories of translation which are blind to the ideological implications of their textual manipulations.[9]

Though traditionally a negative topos in translation, 'difference' becomes a positive one in feminist translation. Like parody, feminist translation is a signifying of difference despite similarity. As feminist theory has been concerned to show, difference is a key factor in cognitive processes and in critical praxis. Meaning discerned and assigned by the translator becomes visible in the gap or the surplus which separates target from source text. (Brisset, 1985: 207). The feminist translator, affirming her critical difference, her delight in interminable re-reading and re-writing, flaunts the signs of her manipulation of the text. *Womanhandling* the text in translation would involve the replacement of the modest, self-effacing translator. Taking her place would be an active participant in the creation of meaning who advances a conditional analysis. Hers is a continuing provisionality, aware of process, giving self-reflexive attention to practices. The feminist translator immodestly flaunts her signature in italics, in footnotes – even in a preface.

Notes

1. Many thanks to Sherry Simon, Lorraine Gauthier and Elizabeth Lamèche for their dialogue.
2. Sandra Harding in a lecture at OISE in February 1983 commented on the feature of feminist discourse, like the discourse of any marginalized group, being characterized by its double or plural perspectives on events, the view from below which was lateral as well as hierarchical, in opposition to the dominant discourse which knew only its own meanings.
3. Subsequent page numbers refer to Lamy (1979).
4. et partir de l'émotion, nuque et ça
   une situation du genre, énoncée
   dans la clarté, les plis, les intuitions
   et s'appliquer pour en être
   au bord et recommencer éprouvée
   toute d'éveil d'être en ses cheveux ouïe. (Brossard, 1985: 22–3)
5. et l'émotion traduire nuque et là
   une dévotion, entendre toute allongée
   dans la clarté tu ris de la façon
   car connaître et rêver au gré
   très tard c'est entamer l'éternité
   d'être en ses cheveuz jouie.
6. This self-translation is the repetition of a process as distinguished from translation of another's work which is reproduction of a product (Fitch, 1985: 117).
7. As Hélène Cixous sums it up, this double-voiced discourse is dis/placement and re/placement, dynamic inter-vention:
   > To admit that writing is precisely working (in) the in-between, inspecting the process of the same *and* of the other without which nothing can live, undoing the work of death – to admit this is first to want the two, as well as both, the ensemble of the one and the other, not fixed in sequences of struggle and expulsion or some other form of death, but infinitely dynamized by an incessant process of exchange from one subject into the other. A process of different subjects knowing one another and beginning one another anew only from the living boundaries of the other: a multiple and inexhaustible course with millions of encounters and transformations of the same into the other and into the in-

between, from which woman takes her forms (and man, in his turn; but that's his other history). (Cixous, 1980: 254)

8. Literary criticism as interpretation, historiography, the prefatory introduction or the book review are other modes of rewriting which shape the evolution of a given literature. Such rewritings operate within constraints, those of patronage, poetics, the universe of discourse and the natural language in which they are written and, in the case of translation, especially, the original work itself (Lefevere, 1985: 235). Translation (and literary) theory would try to explain how these constraints operate and how the interaction of writing and rewriting shapes a given literature.

9. 'La notion de transparence – avec son corollaire moralisé, la "modestie" du traducteur qui s'efface' – appartient à l'opinion, comme ignorance théorique et méconnaissance propre à l'idéologie qui ne se connaît pas elle-même. On lui oppose la traduction comme ré-énonciation spécifique d'un sujet historique, interaction de deux poétiques, décentrement, le dedans-dehors d'une langue et des textualisations dans cette langue (1973: 307–8).

References

Bakhtin, M. M. (1984) *Problems of Dostoevsky's Poetics*, trans. Caryl Emerson; intro. Wayne Booth. Minnesota: University of Minnesota Press.

Bassnett-McGuire, Susan (1980) *Translation Studies*. London: Methuen.

Berman, Antoine (1984) *L' épreuve de l' étranger*. Paris: Gallimard.

Brisset, Annie (1985) 'Transformation para-doxale', *Texte* 4: 205–18.

Brossard, Nicole (1985) *L'Aviva*. Montreal: nbj.

Catford, J. C. (1965) *A Linguistic Theory of Translation: An Essay in Applied Linguistics*. London: Oxford University Press.

Cixous, Hélène (1980) 'The Laugh of the Medusa', trans. Keith and Paula Cohen, in *New French Feminisms*, ed. Elaine Marks and Isabelle de Courtivron. Amherst, MA: University of Massachusetts Press.

Compagnon, Antoine (1979) *La seconde main: ou le travail de la citation*. Paris: Editions du Seuil.

Derrida, Jacques (1978) *Writing and Difference*, trans. Alan Bass. Chicago: University of Chicago Press; 1st published 1967.

Elshtain, Jean Bethke (1982) 'Feminist Discourse and Its Discontents: Language, Power, and Meaning', *Signs* 7(3): 612–28.

Fitch, Brian (1985) 'The Status of Self-Translation', *Texte* 4: 114–22.

Gagnon, Madeleine (1977) 'Mon corps est mots', in *La venue à l' écriture*, ed. Hélène Cixous, Madeleine Gagnon and Annie Leclerc. Paris: 10/18.

Genette, Gérard (1982) *Palimpsestes*. Paris: Editions du Seuil.

Hutcheon, Linda (1981) 'Ironie, satire, parodie', *Poétique* 46: 140–55.

Hutcheon, Linda (1985) *A Theory of Parody: The Teachings of Twentieth-century Art Forms*. London and New York: Methuen.

Irigaray, Luce (1985) *This Sex Which Is Not One*, trans. Catherine Porter. Ithaca, NY. Cornell University Press.

Kemp, Penny (n.d.) *Trance(dance)form*. Victoria: Soft Press.

Lamy, Suzanne (1979) *d'elles*. Montreal: l'hexagone.

Lefevere, Andre (1985) 'Why Waste Our Time on Rewrites? The Trouble with Interpretation and the Role of Rewriting in an Alternative Paradigm', in *The*

Manipulation of Literature. Studies in Literary Translation, ed. Theo Hermans. London: Croom Helm.

Marlatt, Daphne and Nicole Brossard (1985) *Mauve*. Vancouver and Montreal: Writing/nbj.

Marlatt, Daphne and Nicole Brossard (1986) *Character/Jeu de lettres*. Vancouver and Montreal: Writing/nbj.

Meschonnic, Henri (1973) 'Poétique de la traduction', in *Pour la poétique II*. Paris: Gallimard.

Mounin, Georges (1963) *Les problèmes théoriques de la traduction*. Paris: Gallimard.

Payant, René (1979; 1980) 'Bricolage pictural: l'art à propos de l'art. I: Question de la citation. II: Citation et intertextualité', *Parachute* 16; 18: 5–8, 25–32.

Rose, Margaret (1979) *Parody/Metafiction*. London: Croom Helm.

10 Translation and the Mass Media

Dirk Delabastita

This paper deals with the various forms of translation taking place in the international world of audio-visual communication. As yet, little scholarly research has been undertaken in this field. The paper therefore starts with a very concise state of the art report. It further attempts to set up a framework serving the double purpose of providing a unified perspective on what has been done already, as well as suggesting approaches to further research into film.[1]

There is a blatant discrepancy between the obvious importance of translation in the media and the limited attention it has so far been thought worthy of. This discrepancy could easily be expressed in quantitative terms: for many cultures in Europe (not to mention the Third World) a very substantial part, if not most of the mass media messages in circulation have undergone some process of translation. There is, as the following paragraphs may suggest, also a 'qualitative' side to the discrepancy. It is safe to assume that translation processes in mass communication play a very effective part in both the shaping of cultures and the relations between them.

The reasons for this lack of scholarly interest in translation in the media are not far to seek. The social sciences tend to select their objects of study on the basis of cultural prestige, rather than intrinsic interest. It is often thought more prestigious to study Shakespeare than to study popular literature or, for that matter, derivative phenomena such as translations. Those who do study translations would, therefore, rather study translations of Shakespeare than translations of TV soap operas *Sons and Daughters* or *Santa Barbara*.

A second important feature of the discourse on film translation is its highly heterogeneous character. A first and quantitatively largest group of authors on the subject consists of those actively engaged in film translation as professional translators. They provide us with essential first-hand knowledge of the technicalities of film translation and with many useful examples. However, the immediacy of daily practice also makes itself felt in these texts in a less serviceable manner in that they are usually devoted not just to the description, but also to the defence of certain translation practices. Predictably, the discussions usually centre on the dilemma 'dubbing versus subtitling'.[2] In recent years, however, various groups of 'professionals' have published on film translation from a much more detached point of view. There appears to be a growing tendency to analyse translation work on an empirical basis and to take the findings of scientific research into account. Technical developments (cable TV, teletext, satellite TV, video) play an obvious part in this development, as do economic and political pressures. The increasing internationalization of the mass media makes an important 'intensification of television programme imports and exports' (Luyken, 1987: 30) likely. The people in the field will clearly be unable to ignore this development. A major example of this type of 'pragmatic' but highly sophisticated kind of study is the project 'Overcoming Language Barriers in European Television' at the European Institute for the Media, in Manchester.[3]

Many of the claims made in the context of the traditional dubbing vs subtitling debates are based on mere intuition. Some of these intuitions have been tested in experimental psychology. One of the aims of the experiments conducted is to investigate the type and amount of cognitive activity subtitling requires from TV viewers. It appears that the reading of subtitles turns out *not* to require a conscious cognitive effort on the part of those accustomed to this mode of translation. People who read subtitles do not exhibit the typical eye movement patterns of 'ordinary' reading behaviour. Rather, their eyes tend to make no more than a few quick jumps from one keyword to another. The whole process of subtitle perception tends to be largely automatized, so much so that viewers who have no need of subtitles find it hard to avoid reading them.

Contributions to our discussion from the fields of sociology and communication have been relatively minor to date. The most important is Otto Hesse-Quack's monograph *Der Übertragunqsgrozess bei der Synchronisation von Filmen* (1969).[4] The study claims that mass communication acts both as a 'reflector' and as a 'moulder' of the values, norms, stereotypes and attitudes of a given society. Translation acts like a 'gatekeeper' and, accordingly, the shifts introduced by the dubbing process in the imported film material can be studied as evidence of the differences between the respective *Symbolmilieus* of source and target culture. Many such shifts appear to occur, and some are of a rather sweeping nature: slang and dialect usually disappear; social criticism tends to be toned down, obscenity is filtered out, as are references to homosexuality. Other cultures are made the butt of jokes; criticism of certain aspects of German culture and allusions to the Nazi period are carefully excised. Film translation is therefore not just a matter of language conversion, and the actual reality of film translation is conditioned to a large extent by the functional needs of the receiving culture and not, or not just, by the demands made by the source films.[5]

In spite of its broad title, Istvan Fodor's essay *Film Dubbing: Phonetic, Semiotic, Esthetic and Psychological Aspects* concentrates mainly on the phonetic side of the film dubbing problem. Fodor calls for the further development of a new discipline: 'visual phonetics', next to the existing disciplines of acoustic and auxiliary phonetics. The discipline's central problem is that of the analysis of the process of deriving linguistically relevant information from merely looking at a speaker. This issue is obviously tied in closely with the notorious problem of sound/image synchronicity in dubbing. The pronunciation of different languages obviously has a different visual impact. These differences are caused not only by strictly phonological features, but also by the divergence between various paralinguistic and gestural patterns, such as facial expressions and body language.

The study of film translation appears to require an interdisciplinary effort, including specific contributions by film and TV professionals, psychologists and psycholinguists, mass-communication experts, phoneticians, sociolinguists, film semioticians and translation scholars. Yet the latter have almost completely neglected the field up to now. It is not very hard to see why this should be so. In the first place, many scholars have so far preferred to devote their energy to the development of a theory of translation. Their bias is often so strongly theoretical and their models turn out to be so abstract that there is hardly any room left for the empirical study of actual translations, and certainly of translations in the field of mass communication. ('Think of the notorious debates on the notion of 'translatability' at a time when more translations are being made than ever before.)

Secondly, subtitling and dubbing are often governed by the respective constraints of text compression and lip synchronicity. In many cases these constraints occupy a higher position in the translator's hierarchy of priorities than do considerations of syntax, style or lexicon. This fact is taken implicitly as sufficient motivation for qualifying film translation as a form of 'adaptation' rather than 'translation proper' and for excluding it from the research domain of translation studies.

Yet the new approach to translation studies characterized by Theo Hermans could prove a useful point of departure for the study of film translation. Hermans' point of departure is:

[A] view of literature as a complex and dynamic system; a conviction that there should be a continual interplay between theoretical models and practical case-studies; an approach to literary translation which is descriptive, target-oriented, functional and systemic; and an interest in the norms and constraints that govern the production and reception of translations, in the relation between translation and other types of text processing, and in the place and role of translations both within a given literature and in the interaction between literatures. (Hermans, 1985: 10–11)

The historical-descriptive, polysystemic, structural-semiotic hypotheses referred to have so far mainly been tested in the field of literary translation.[6] In what follows I shall attempt to sketch a methodology for a possible application of the hypotheses in question to film translation.

The researcher in the field of film translation should, of course, first delimit the target system corpus s/he intends to work with. S/he should then proceed to establish the principles governing the very presence/absence of imported and translated film material in the cultural system under discussion. In Gideon Toury's terminology, s/he should try first to establish the *preliminary norms* governing translation in the target system. These preliminary norms '[H]ave to do with two sets of considerations: those regarding the very existence of a translation "policy" along with its actual nature, and those questions related to the "directness" of translation' (Toury, 1980: 53).

Toury lists the following 'considerations regarding translation policy':

[T]he factors affecting or determining the choice of works (or at least of authors, genres, schools, source literatures [*sic*], and the like) to be translated. Let us say that such a policy (that is, a norm-regulated choice) exists when the determining factors are found to be systematic and patterned, and not merely accidental. (1980: 53)

The questions to be asked, then, are: what is the relative share of translated films in the total supply of the target system? Does the relative presence of film import vary according to particular subsystems within the corpus (genre, cinema vs. TV, different circuits in the world of cinema)? Is there a significant preference for/resistance against import from particular languages/cultures, genres, schools?

The Low Countries, for instance, have a very high percentage of film import. No less than 40 per cent of all BRT (Belgian Radio and Television) programmes are of foreign origin and need to be translated (Muylaert et al., 1982), and this rate is still higher in the cinema circuit. In France, on the other hand, the percentage of imported films is much lower, and is even subject to official regulations. Importing films is still fairly exceptional in the United States, especially if the films have been produced in non-English-speaking source cultures. Home-made remakes are often preferred to foreign imports, as recently attested by the very successful remake of *Three Men and a Baby*.

Toury's second set of preliminary considerations concerns directness of translation. What is the degree of tolerance towards film
translations made on the basis of an intermediary translation, rather
than the actual source film? Is this potential degree of tolerance
restricted to particular original source languages and/or to particular
intermediary languages? When the source film is made in some
'exotic' small language, intermediate translation is often standard
practice. But its application is not restricted to such more or less
exceptional cases. In Belgian cinema translation many films are
provided with double (i.e. bilingual) subtitles. The Dutch subtitles
quite often appear to be a translation of the French subtitles, rather
than 'direct' translations of the original dialogues.

I believe we should add a third set of preliminary considerations,
not mentioned by Toury. In the case of a multilingual target system,
the researcher should establish which of the language(s) is/are
selected for translation, and whether there may be parameters
governing this selection. In the Walloon (French-speaking) part of
Belgium, cinemas usually screen feature films in the dubbed version
produced in France. Cinemas in Brussels show either the same
dubbed versions or the original versions with bilingual subtitles, and
these are often the versions shown in Flanders as well. Similarly, TV
programmes may undergo a double translation process in the Basque
part of Spain: dialogues are dubbed in Basque, but the screen also
shows Spanish subtitles. Technical innovations (teletext, stereo TV)
sometimes allow viewers to make their own selection, or to combine
various translated versions as they please.

The issue of the use of various possible techniques of film translation is greatly complicated by the particular semiotic nature of the
total film sign. Three important features appear to be especially
relevant here:

(1) Film communication usually proceeds through two channels:
the visual channel (light waves) and the acoustic channel (air vibra-
tions).

(2) There is a multitude of codes that shape a film into a complex
meaningful sign: the verbal code (an aggregate of various linguistic
and paralinguistic sub-codes), narrative codes, vestimentary codes,
moral codes, cinematic codes.

(3) As a product of mass communication, the transmission and
manipulation of films and fragments of films is subject to certain
technical restrictions.

On the basis of these distinctions, the researcher is able to differen-
tiate between four types of film sign: verbal signs transmitted acoustically (dialogue), non-verbal signs transmitted acoustically (back-

ground noise, music), verbal signs transmitted visually (credits, letters, documents shown on the screen), non-verbal signs transmitted visually. These four categories of film signs will constitute one axis of film translation. The other axis will specify exactly what type of operation is involved. To specify these types of operation I shall make use of the following categories of classical rhetoric: *repetitio, adiectio, detractio, substitutio* and *transmutatio*.

Traditionally, the two basic techniques of film translation are dubbing (*substitutio* of acoustic/verbal signs) and subtitling (*adiectio* of visual/verbal signs). Yet the researcher should not be blind to certain other techniques which may occur either as an alternative to these basic techniques or in combination with them:

Detractio: visual and/or acoustic and verbal and/or non-verbal signs have been deleted (cuts).

Repetitio: the film has been reproduced with all of its original material features; (in strict linguistic terms this would be a case of non-translation).

Adiectio: new images, sounds, dialogue or spoken comments have been introduced.

The selection of a film translation technique does not exhaust the range of choices open to the translator. In describing the relationship between original and translated films, the researcher will therefore have to consider a further set of questions. S/he will be able to draw upon the descriptive apparatus evolved by mainstream translation studies to achieve this. Special attention should be paid to:

—the rendering of particular language varieties, whether local (dialect), social (register, jargon) or personal (idiosyncracies, speech defects and the like); this issue requires special attention in the case of subtitling, since most subtitles involve a shift from a spoken to a written variety of language.

—the rendering of literary allusions (quotations, allusions, parody) and of various cultural data (conventions, habits and items typical of the local sociocultural environment).

—the potentially different treatment of various special types of verbal message: character speech versus narrator speech, flashbacks, letters being written/read, musical texts, background conversation, peritextual signs such as titles and credits.

—the rendering of wordplay and other forms of humorous language use.

—the rendering of taboo elements.

—the rendering of prosodic features.

—the translator's attitude towards loan words and foreign idioms as well as the presence of linguistic interference in general.

—the possible introduction of genre markers, i.e. stereotyped elements that further conform the target film to the target audience's expectations.

In addition, the description should take into account that certain shifts may have occurred on the film's macrotextual level: segmentation of the text, narrative structure, plot, characters. There are many cases in which the film translator has directly introduced shifts on these levels. It should also be remembered that the total effect of a series of microstructural shifts may just as well amount to a significant shift on the macrostructural level.

Since films can be translated in various ways, film translation constitutes a typical situation in which *norms* can be expected to guide the selection of actual behaviour in each historical set of circumstances. In Gideon Toury's words:

[T]here is a point in assuming the existence of norms only in situations which in principle allow for several variations of behavior. Such variations are either meaningless, being a case of free variation, or patterned, that is directed and regulated by norms (being, as it were, cases of 'bound variation'). . . . Therefore, inasmuch as a norm is really active and effective, one can distinguish regularity of behavior in recurrent situations of the same type. It is only natural that such regularities should serve as the main evidence in the *study* of norms as well. (1980· 51–2)[7]

A description of film translation should therefore not consist of an accumulation of atomistic analyses. Only the systematic observation of entire series of translations will allow the researcher to establish the normative principles truly governing audience behaviour. The following questions will have to be asked:

What is the position of the target culture in an international context? Is it prestigious or peripheral? Does it entertain frequent relations with the source culture or with other cultures?

What is the position of the source culture in an international context? Does it enjoy high prestige or is it perceived as a minor culture, relatively devoid of interest?

Does the target audience impose particular restrictions on the translator in terms of literacy (films for children, for instance, for seniors, for immigrants, films shown in the context of literacy campaigns)?

Which text-type does the source film belong to? Is it a text-type that basically attempts to communicate information (facts) or is its primary goal entertainment or artistic effect (fiction)?

Since it is impossible to define text-types ahistorically, the previous question might be rephrased as follows: which historical genre does the source film belong to (documentary, news report, western)? The distinction between cinema and TV genres may well become important at this point. The larger problem of genre raises further potentially relevant questions:

Does the genre the source film belongs to exist in the receiving culture? Do the source film's models (linguistic, stylistic, cultural, filmic) find a counterpart in the target culture?

Are we dealing with a genre in which the qualities of the vocal performance are believed to be an integral part of the entire artistic sign? Think of filmed versions of famous theatre performances, opera-films, musicals.

What cultural status does the source film genre claim? In Flanders, for instance, the BBC Shakespeare for Television series was not subtitled by a member of the BRT subtitling crew, but by the country's foremost Shakespeare translator, Willy Courteaux.

Does the source film claim a particular status within the genre to which it belongs? Many of Walt Disney's films, for instance, belong to the genre of the animated cartoon or the children's movie, but they may well receive different translational treatment on account of the special, canonical status they have acquired within both genres.

Judging from these lists of questions, there is not much point in looking for one single norm which supposedly governs 'the' transla-tion of film texts in general. Rather, we shall have to try to identify a complex group of more or less interrelated norms. Some of the normative principles governing film translation in a corpus under study may well have nothing to do with either 'translation' or 'film' in the strict sense of both words. This is not altogether a surprising conclusion for the researcher who is willing to accept that cultures are phenomena constructed in complex ways, or 'polysystems'. It is to be expected that the norms which will emerge as relevant to film translation will be linked to the following elements, at least:

Concepts of genre within the target film and TV system: what does a good news report, or a good soap opera look like? What are the current norms and opinions on the relative value and function of 'image' and 'spoken word' in the artistic unity of films? Are there certain canonical models?

The linguistic organization of the target culture: what varieties, registers, styles does the target language have at its disposal, and how do they relate to each other? How do written and spoken language relate to each other? Which attitudes are adopted towards neighbour-ing or 'exotic' languages (openness versus purism)? Which foreign language teaching policy has been adopted?

The literary organization of the target culture: what are the literary categories and textual models the target culture uses to organize its experiences?

What degree of openness does the target culture display towards other cultures? Does it entertain relations of dominance, subordina-tion, competition – or any relations at all? Does the target culture constitute a stable system or does it find itself in a period of rapid change?

What is the dominant concept of translation in other fields, such as literary translation, translation in the printed mass media, technical translation?

It is my basic hypothesis that at least some of these features are needed to understand both the variables and the constant factors in actual film translation. This hypothesis has far-reaching implications. For one, it becomes impossible to maintain that translation studies can legitimately refuse to enter into a dialogue with a broad range of other disciplines. It becomes equally impossible to think that a researcher can study film translation (or any other kind of translation, for that matter) in isolation from the cultural contexts in which it is practised – and vice versa. In fact, if the relations between translation and culture really are of the intrinsic nature suggested here, there may well be nothing outside translation.

Notes

1. For the sake of verbal economy I shall use the term 'film' in an unusually encompassing sense. 'Film' will therefore be taken to include TV programmes as well. Wherever the distinction between TV and film is relevant to my argument, it will be made explicit.
2. The current arguments are well known. Defenders of dubbing claim that subtitles destroy the original photography and that they are economically unjustifiable (they turn off audiences), socially unjustifiable (they appeal to intellectuals only) and artistically unjustifiable (production costs are much higher). Defenders of subtitling in turn claim that dubbing destroys the original soundtrack, that it is economically unjustifiable (production costs are much higher), socially unjustifiable (viewers are deprived of the occasion to improve their linguistic competence) and artistically unjustifiable (for various reasons). Subtitles allow the translator more leeway, they take less time to make and they disrupt neither the cultural/linguistic nor the body/voice coherence of the original film. On the other hand, it is claimed that subtitling demands a considerable amount of cognitive effort on the part of the viewer/reader.
3. Similar initiatives have been taken elsewhere. There is a one-year postgraduate course in film and TV translation at the University of Lille, France. Professional organizations of film translators such as the French Association Cinéma Traduction are gaining in importance. Both the Fédération Internationale des Traducteurs and the European Broadcasting Union are taking an increased interest in film translation.
4. The References section which follows this paper is designed to do double duty, both as a list of works cited and as an introductory bibliography designed to aid prospective researchers in the field.
5. In these important respects Hesse-Quack's book anticipates the view of film translation that will be presented in this paper. Yet there are also important differences. Hesse-Quack's concept of culture appears rather static in nature: both

source and target culture are viewed as essentially homogeneous (rather than polyphonic) and relatively free from historical change (rather than dynamic). Hesse-Quack therefore regards translation shifts between source and target films as mere *indicators* of cultural *differences*. I believe they can actually be studied as *agents* of intercultural *evolution*.

6. Hermans contains a representative selection of case studies and provides further bibliographical references. There is an obvious historical explanation for the basic orientation of the 'new paradigm' towards literary translation. Polysystems theory has not simply developed from a dissatisfaction with older research schemes in translation studies; it is also – especially – to be understood as the result of conceptual and methodological evolutions within the (comparative) study of literature. Historically, the 'new paradigm' could be called a symbiotic association of new trends both in translation studies and in the study of literature.

7. Toury also mentions the existence of a second source for the study of translational norms: 'semi-theoretical or critical formulations, such as prescriptive theories (or poetics) of translation, statements made by translators, editors, publishers, and other persons involved in or connected with translation, in public as well as in private, critical appraisals of single translations, and so forth' (Toury, 1980: 57). Even though such formulations always have to be treated with caution, they can also be used in the case of film translation, in the guise of audience evaluation surveys, for instance.

References

Auboyer, D. and R. Paillez (1977) 'Sous-titres et sous-titrage', *La Revue du Cinema* 314 (Feb.).

Baetens Beardsmore, H. (ed.) (1984) 'Language and Television', *International Journal of the Sociology of Language* 84.

Baetens Beardsmore, H. and H. van Beeck (1984) 'Multilingual Television Supply and Language Shift', *International Journal of the Sociology of Language* 84: 65–80.

Baker, R. G. (1981) *Guidelines for the Subtitling of Television Programmes for the Deaf and Hard of Hearing*. Southampton: Southampton University.

Baker, R. G., A. D. Lambourne and G. Rowston (1984) *Handbook for Television Subtitlers*, rev. ed. Winchester: IBA Engineering Division.

Borges, J. L. (1982) 'Over Nasynchronisatie', *Literair Paspoort* 22: 107–8.

Braem, H. M. (1968) 'Übersetzer und Fernsehen', *Der Übersetzer* 5 (2): 4.

Caille, P.-Fr. (1960) 'Cinema et traduction', *Babel* 6: 103–9.

Caille, P.-Fr. (1965) 'La traduction au cinéma', in *Übersetzen. Vorträge und Beiträge vom internationalen Kongress literarischer Übersetzer in Hamburg*, ed. R. Italiaander. Hamburg: Athenaum: 116–22.

Caille, P.-Fr. (1967) 'La traduction au cinema', *Le Linguiste/De Taalkundige* 13: 5–6, 1–4.

Cary, E. (1956) 'La traduction cinématographique', in *La traduction dans le monde moderne*. Geneva: Georg: 105–13.

Cary, E. (1960) 'La traduction totale', *Babel* 6: 110–15.

Cary, E. (1985) 'Comment s'effectue le doublage cinématographique?', in *Comment faut-il traduire?*, Introduction, bibliography and index by Michel Ballard. Presses Universitaires de Lille: 65–71.

Chion, M. (1982) *La Voix au cinéma*. Paris: L'etoile.
'Cinema et traduction'. (1960) Special issue of *Babel* 6.
Comstock, G. et al. (1978) *Television and Human Behaviour*. New York: Columbia University Press.
Curtis, J.-L. (1986) 'Traduire, c'est trahir', *Télérama* 1919 (22 Oct.): 69–70.
Delabastita, D. (1988) 'Translation and Mass-Communication. Film and TV Translation as Evidence of Cultural Dynamics'. Leuven: KUL Catholic University of Louvain Departement Literatuurwetenschap.
Delmas, Chr. (1978) 'Les traductions synchrones', in *La traduction, une profession*. Ottawa: Conseil des traducteurs et interprètes du Canada: 22, 413–19.
D'Haeyer, W. (1964) 'Film en TV-adaptatie en-vertaling', *Le Linguiste/De Taalkundige* 10 (6): 13.
D'Haeyer, W. (1968) 'Moelijkheden bij de vertaling van TV,-films', *Le Linguiste/De Taalkundige* 14 (14): 5.
Dollerup, C. (1974) 'On Subtitling in Television Programmes', *Babel* 20: 197–202.
d'Ydewalle, G., P. Muylle and J. van Rensbergen (1985) 'Attention Shifts in Partially Redundant Information Situations', *Eye Movement and Human Information Processing*, ed R. Groner et al. 375–84.
d'Ydewalle, G. and J. van Rensbergen (1986) 'Developmental Studies of Text–Picture Interactions in the Perception of Animated Cartoons with Text'. Leuven: KUL Laboratory of Experimental Psychology.
d'Ydewalle, G., J. Van Rensburgen and J. Pollet (1987) 'Reading a Message when the Same Message is Available Auditorily in Another Language: the Case of Subtitling', in *Eye Movements from Physiology to Cognition*, ed J. O. Regan and A. Levy-Schoen. Amsterdam: Elsevier North-Holland: 313–21.
d'Ydewalle, G., L. Warlop and J. Van Rensbergen (1987) 'Verschillen tussen jonge en oudere volwassenen in de verdeling van de aandacht over verschillende informatiebronnen'. Leuven: KUL Laboratory of Experimental Psychology.
Even-Zohar, I. and G. Toury (eds) (1981) 'Translation Theory and Intercultural Relations', *Poetics Today* 2.
Fodor, I. (1969) 'Linguistic and Psychological Problems of Film Synchronisation', *Acta Linguistica Academiae Scientiarum Hungaricae* 19: 69–106, 379–94.
Fodor, I. (1976) *Film Dubbing: Phonetic, Semiotic, Esthetic and Psychological Aspects*. Hamburg: Buske.
Gautier, G.-L. (1981) 'La traduction au cinema: nécessité et trahison', *La Revue du Cinéma* 363 (May–Aug.).
Gorlich, E. J. (1967) 'Italienische Filme in deutscher Betitelung', *Idioma* 4: 31–3.
Groen, M. (1975) 'Films vertalen is schipperen', *Skoop* 2: 9.
Hermans, Th. (ed.) (1985) *The Manipulation of Literature. Studies in Literary Translation*. London and Sydney: Croom.
Hesse-Quack, O. (1969) *Der Übertragingsprozess bei der Synchronisation von Filmen. Eine interkulturelle Untersuchung*. Munich/Basle: Reinhardt.
Holmberg, A. (s.d.) *Subtitling of Television Programmes. New Methods for the Hard-of-hearing*. Sveriges Television, Teletext Department.
Horguelin, P. A. (ed.) (1978) *La traduction, une profession/Translating, a Profession, Actes du VIIIe Congrès mondiale de la FIT*. Ottawa: Conseil des traducteurs et interprètes du Canada.
Just, M. A. and P. A. Carpenter (1986) *The Psychology of Reading and Language Comprehension*. Boston: Allyn and Bacon.

Lambert, J. (1983) 'Un modèle descriptif pour la description de la littérature. La littérature comme polysysteme'. Leuven: KUL, Afdeling Algemene Literatuurwetenschap.

L'Anglais, P. (1960) 'Le doublage, art difficile', *Journal des Traducteurs* 5(4): 109–13.

Lardeau, Y. (1982) 'Les voix artificielles du cinema', *Théâtre Public*: 44, 68–70.

Luyken, G. (1987) 'In Other Words', *Cable and Satellite Europe* 5 30–4; 6: 57–61.

Malm, J. (1983) 'Translation for TV and How We Do It in Sweden', *Actes du 9ème Congrès mondial de la F.I.T.* (Warsaw, 1981): 405–8.

Marleau, L. (1982) 'Les sous-titres . . . un mal nécessaire', *Meta* 27(3): 271–85.

Milosz, A. (1983) 'Traduction et adaptation de textes filmiques destinés aux besoins de la cinématographie', *Actes du 9ème Congrès mondial de la F.I.T.* (Warsaw, 1981): 352–6.

Minchinton, J. (1987) 'Fitting Titles', *Sight & Sound* 56 (4): 279–82.

Moulaert, P. (1962) 'La langue des opéras', *Le Linguiste/De taalkundige* 4: 10–11.

Mounin, G. (1967) *Die Übersetzung. Geschichte, Theorie, Anwendung*. Munich: Nymphenburg.

Muylaert, W., J. Nootens, D. Poesmans and A. K. Pugh (1982) *Perceptie van ondertitels bij anderstalige televisieprogramma's*. Brussels: BRT–studiedienst.

Muylaert, W., J. Nootens, D. Poesmans and A. K. Pugh (1983) 'Design and Utilisation of Subtitles on Foreign Language Television Programmes', in *Théorie, Methoden und Modelle der Kontaktlinguistik*, ed. P. H. Nelde. Bonn: Dummler: 201–14.

Myers, L. (1973) 'The Art of Dubbing', *Filmmakers' Newsletter* 6 (6): 56–8.

Neve, M. de (1985) 'En bovendien vertalen ze niet alles!', *Taalbeheersing in de praktijk* 212.

Nir, R. (1984) 'Linguistic and Sociolinguistic Problems in the Translation of Imported TV Films in Israel', *International Journal of the Sociology of Language* 84: 91–7.

Noel, Cl. (1970) 'Le doublage de films', *Traduire* 64: 3–10.

NOS, *De behoeften van doven en slechthorenden aan ondertiteling van Nederlandse televisieprogramma's*. Research Rep. R77 0 194. Hilversum (The Netherlands).

Reid, H. (1978) 'Sub-titling, the Intelligent Solution', in *La traduction, une profession*, ed. P. A. Horguelin. Ottawa: Conseil des traducteurs et interprètes du Canada: 420–8.

Reid, H. (1983) 'The Translator on the Screen', *Actes du 9ème Congrès mondial de la F.I.T.* (Warsaw, 1981): 357–9.

Reiss, K. (1971) *Möglichkeiten und Grenzen der Übersetzungskritik*. Munich: Max Huber.

Rose, T. C. (1960) 'The English Dubbing Text', *Babel* 6: 116–20.

Salomon, G. (1979) *Interaction of Media, Cognition and Learning*. San Francisco, CA: Jossey-Bass.

Schochat, E. and R. Stam (1985) 'The Cinema after Babel: Language, Difference and Power', *Screen* 26: 3–4.

'Stockholm 87–Conference de l'UER sur le doublage et le sous-titrage', *Revue de l'UER* (1987) 38 (6): 8–31.

Toury, G. (1980) *In Search of a Theory of Literary Translation*. Tel Aviv: Porter Institute for Poetics and Semiotics.

Verfaillie, K. and G. d'Ydewalle (1987) 'Modality Preference and Message Comprehension in Deaf Youngsters Watching T.V.', Leuven: KUL Laboratory of Experimental Psychology.

Voge, H. (1977) 'The Translation of Films: Sub-titling versus Dubbing', *Babel* 23: 120–5.

Warlop, L., J. van Rensbergen and G. d'Ydewalle (1986) 'Ondertiteling op de BRT. Leuven: KUL Laboratory of Experimental Psychology.

Welleman, G. (1969) The Principles and Procedure of Film Translation and More Particularly of English–French Subtitle Translation', Unpublished dissertation, KUL.

Wermeskerken, S. van (1956) 'Filmvertaalperikelen', *Van taal tot taal* 1: (1): 8–10.

[Anon] (1956) 'Traduction et cinéma', *Le linguiste/De taalkundige* 1: 5, 10.

11 Translating the Will to Knowledge: Prefaces and Canadian Literary Politics

Sherry Simon

The close historical relationship between translation and literary rhetoric might once have seemed like a major obstacle in conceptualizing translation history. How can the historical specificity of translation be isolated when there seems to be so much repetition and sheer falsehood in the discourse on translation, when dense thickets of topoi spring up at every turn? How can we attempt to valorize translation when translators have for centuries defined their work in terms of the most conservative literary values of their age?

In fact these disadvantages have become sources of new interest over the last few years as translation history devotes itself not to writing a linear chronology of translation events but to articulating translation to the diverse writing practices and values engaged in specific contexts. The intense relationship between translation and axiology then becomes interesting in itself. We come to understand the 'translator' as traversed and indeed constituted by the various discourses which define literature and its functions in a particular historical context (Guillerm, 1984: 59).

Paratextual elements in translations – the peripheral matter which accompanies the texts of translations – are useful tools in analysing the constructed subject of translation in its various historical forms. Of particular interest are the signature (the name of the translator) and the preface (the word of the translator). The name of the translator, for instance, like the name of the author, as Michel Foucault (1977: 124) has shown, is a sign which has historically variable functions. For example: the 'author' takes on historically specific functions as an element of explanation in critical discourse; it is used in different ways in the physical presentation of books and bibliographies and in library classification; the legal and copyright provisions associated with authorship are constantly evolving. Similarly the 'translator' takes on context-specific meaning; we can follow the history of the name of the translator by identifying the way in which it appears physically in books (which translations carried the name of the translator) as well as in critical discourse and in the changing legal provisions given the translator in copyright law (Simon, forthcoming).

As for prefaces, their content and function have yet to be analysed systematically. Their very presence and frequency at different periods is an indication of the prominence given to the translator: the preface foregrounds the presence of the second hand. And it is significant that much of what has been said about translation until recently has been said in prefaces – that is in a context where the focus on immediate readership is foremost.

Often rejected outright by literary historians as fabrics of topoi or as texts too directly linked to the political and commercial sponsors of translations, prefaces now seem interesting precisely because of their hybrid role. Since the Middle Ages the preface has spoken a double language – it is at the same time speech and action. Offering information, it also seeks protection from the outrages of power; advancing propitiatory disclaimers, it also propels the work towards new markets and audiences. It seeks above all to capture the goodwill of the public, as its Latin name the *captatio benevolentia* emphasized. But although some of the terms of this attempt have remained astonishingly stable since the Middle Ages, others have changed dramatically.

I will briefly outline a few elements defining the translator's preface as a historical genre and then look at the preface in the context of the translated novel in Canada – where prefaces have taken on a very specific ideological role.

Taking the Translator's Word for it

Analysis of prefaces inevitably focuses on the distance between their respective meanings and their effective function. Serge Lusignan in his important study of translators' prefaces in the thirteenth and fourteenth centuries in France notes the insistent repetition of a limited number of themes as well as clear indications of the essential political role given to translation (Lusignan, 1986: 129–71). Luce Guillerm in her study of a corpus of 120 prefaces between 1530 and 1560 in France notes as well the overwhelming 'poverty' of their discourse and points to the real receptor of the prefaces – the dedicatee – as the essential clue to the importance of the translation: translations of classical works were dedicated to the king; translations of vernacular works were dedicated to a female member of the royal family. The textual hierarchy mirrors gender values (Guillerm, 1980: 28).

One might think that the ritual nature of prefaces concerns only the pre-modern period, the period preceding what Antoine Compagnon (1979: 235ff.) calls the 'immobilisation of the text' during the Classical period. But José Lambert also underscores the unreliable nature of prefaces during the Romantic period. Criticizing an article which uses a good number of translators' prefaces to prove that there has been a historical change in the manner of translating, Lambert argues that neither Mme de Staël, nor Chateaubriand, nor Emile Deschamps, Amédée Pichot or Mme de Rochmondet are to be 'taken at their word'. The critic must be on guard against their words, he says: 'they mark the significant distance, well-known to translation specialists, between words and actions' (Lambert, 1975: 397; my translation).

What is particularly untrustworthy about translators and why are their words so suspicious? One possible answer to this question is of particular interest to our Canadian case and it is the following. At different moments in history, translations have been particularly closely linked to national political aspirations and prefaces are a revelation of this link. This has been shown clearly for the Middle Ages and the Renaissance. The political dimensions inherent in translation were obvious as well to the Romantics. The extremely violent reception which the Italians gave Mme de Staël's 'Letter on the Spirit of Translations' in 1816 is ample proof that national sensibilities were deeply touched by her appeal to translation (de Staël, 1820). If Mme de Staël ostensibly recommended translation as a means for the Italians to rediscover a new sense of national self-affirmation, many Italians understood this friendly advice as an insult. The complex relationship between translation, literature and national sensibilities became a central concern of the new discipline of comparative literature in the last years of the nineteenth century and the beginning of the twentieth (see particularly Hazard, 1921 *passim*). The early comparatists clearly recognized the fact that translations serve national interests.

Rather than dismissing prefaces for being too closely linked to political imperatives, I would like to suggest that they be read precisely at this level. In addition to revealing the historically shifting relationship between author and translator and foregrounding the foundations of literary values, prefaces are useful precisely because they trace the contours of literary ideology and expose for us the sociopolitical context which commands literary exchanges.

The 'True' Quebec

Literary translation in Canada is a relatively recent phenomenon, in comparison with European standards. The first translated novels date from the middle of the nineteenth century and translations came in isolated bunches until they took off in the 1960s and especially from 1972 onwards, when literary translation became supported financially by the federal government. Historically English-Canadians have been more interested in translating Quebec novels than the opposite, although there have been periods – including the present – when the reverse has been true. English-Canadians have also much more readily written prefaces for their works (about three English prefaces for one French one).

During the period from 1865 to 1950, a significant number of English-language prefaces explicitly place literary translation within the larger context of the political relationship between English and French Canada. An exemplary preface in this regard is that written in 1890 by Charles G. D. Roberts, a prominent English-Canadian writer, to his translation of a novel called *The Canadians of Old* by Philippe Aubert de Gaspé (Aubert de Gaspé, 1974: 5–8). This is an important translation, one which was to become a classic, and which has been frequently re-edited under different titles and with different prefatory material. (Along with *Canadians of Old*, and *Seigneur d'Haberville*, it was also given the somewhat misleading title *Cameron of Lochiel*.) In this preface Roberts makes two assumptions which were to ground literary translation in Canada from then on: (1) the French-Canadian novel is a 'faithful depiction' of life and sentiment among early French Canadians; though a 'literary work' it also has important documentary value; and (2) therefore literary translation is a vehicle through which one constituent of the Canadian collectivity can acquire knowledge of the other. 'In Canada there is settling into shape a nation of two races; there is springing into existence, at the same time, a literature in two languages ... We of English speech (he says) turn naturally to French-Canadian literature for knowledge of the French-Canadian people' (Aubert de Gaspé, 1974: 5).

History, literature and politics are joyfully mingled here in a first definition of the vocation of literary translation in Canada. Magnanimous overtures to the literature and society of French Canada stand next to somewhat condescending references to the 'extravagant dreams of French Canadian nationalism' and its 'not unworthy determination to keep intact its speech and institutions'. Roberts also recalls that *Canadians of Old*, which recounts the events of the conquest of French Canada by Britain, has a passage in which the dying Seigneur advises his son to serve the king of England.

In translators' prefaces to English versions of Quebec novels of the first half of the twentieth century, several of the themes which Roberts evoked are repeated. Rivard (1924) says of a series of tableaux by Adjutor Rivard that 'it lays bare for us the generous and kindly. French-Canadian heart'; Ferres (1925) says of the tales of Brother Marie-Victorin that they offer 'a more intimate knowledge of the literature and mental attitude of our French-speaking fellow citizens, leading to a more fully cordial entente': the Walters say of *Thirty Acres* (Ringuet, 1940) that it is the 'most authentic account of rural French Canada since *Maria Chapdelaine*', and Alan Sullivan (Savard, 1947) believes that *Menaud, maître draveur* 'may be taken as expressing the resilient, fanciful and spontaneous spirit of most of our French-Canadian patriots'. The translators evoke the hope that better knowledge of French Canada will lead to a better political relationship between the two collectivities. Although couched in less naive language, many contemporary prefaces continue to note the social and political context which is the main impulse for translation in Canada.

Prefaces to French-language translations of English-Canadian works are rarer and quite different in tone. Take for example the preface to the translation by Pamphile Lemay of a historical novel, *The Golden Dog* by William Kirby. The translation was published in 1884, so is almost contemporary with Robert's 1890 preface. This preface is written not by the translator but by the publisher who in responding to the question – why have we translated this book? – replies in three points: (1) The book pays superb homage to our French-Canadian ancestors, all the more so because it was written by a man 'belonging by blood and belief' to a nation which was our long-time enemy; (2) We wish to have our literature profit from the admirable work which this man created out of our very own history; (3) Even though the author is a Protestant, he has a sense of religion far stronger than those so-called Catholic authors who attack the Church. All the same, the editor must admit that a few expressions which were not consistent with the Catholic faith were modified.

What dominates in this preface is the immense weight of cultural difference. The foreign and potentially hostile origin of the author is often recalled. While the preface insists on the representational and authentically historical nature of the work (as Roberts does), it stresses the fact that this image of Quebec's own reality has been rendered by a foreigner. The principal interest of the work is the understanding of this image of oneself that has been drawn through alien eyes. This theme is oft-repeated until about 1955. In fact, in examining the relatively limited corpus of translations into French in Quebec until 1950, one is struck by the large number of works – fictional and non-fictional – which are about Quebec itself. Until very recently, then, Quebec has translated images of itself rendered by others; English Canada on the other hand has used translation to discover the clue to the mysteries of Quebec. We see then that if these prefaces use similar terms to describe the usefulness of translations, the terms are not used symmetrically. Roberts is translating a representation of French Canada for the English; Pamphile Lemay is also translating a representation of French Canada, but for the French.

Prefaces in Canadian translations have clearly focused on the collective context. They define the 'knowledge' which translations are supposed to furnish in terms of the specific needs of the group. The decision of the Canadian government to fund literary translation is therefore quite congruent with the perspective in which translation has been carried out in English Canada from the start – literary translation is carried out within explicitly social and political parameters.

Literary Values

The obvious question now is – what impact do these pronouncements have on the translations themselves? Is there in the works themselves the same convergence of practice as in the prefaces? With this question we return to one of the questions we began with: is the word of the translator to be taken seriously?

We have already remarked that when Charles G. D. Roberts defined literary translation as a vehicle for 'knowledge' he defines this knowledge within strict parameters. Translations are to provide for English-Canadian readers an authentic representation of French-Canadian life and thought. This does not mean automatically however that translators adopt an ethnographic approach respectful of the culturally alien origin of the material. On the contrary, as the comparison between Roberts' own version and that of a succeeding translator–editor Thomas Marquis shows, Roberts' version is a classically 'ethnocentric' and 'hypertextual' translation – to use Antoine Berman's terms (1985: 48–9) – while Marquis added footnotes and stayed much closer to the text in order to give the work more of a documentary value. The same cleavage is seen in the two simultaneous translations of *Maria Chapdelaine* by two translators, W. H. Blake and Andrew MacPhail, in 1921. One translation exhibits the values of elegance and the supplement of style; the other remains conscientiously transparent and permeable to the specific structures and features of the French.

That the hypertextual translations have become the consecrated texts within the Canadian literary canon is evidence that aesthetic considerations have won out over ethnographic ones. But the presence of the second, alternative, translations points to a tension in Canadian translation. The 'will to knowledge' that translation is to convey is by no means univocal. If translators are unanimous in understanding translation in Canada as a necessarily collective endeavour, they are less clear about the way in which this knowledge is to be materialized.

The much larger translation corpuses produced in English Canada and Quebec since 1950 have of course substantially broadened the schematic terms which once commanded translations. While some translators' prefaces continue to delineate the sociopolitical parameters of Canadian literary translation, new terms have emerged in areas such as feminist translation.

Until quite recently English-Canadian and Quebec literature have pursued entirely parallel paths; translation has been limited entirely to a role of mediation. Translated works have not been involved in cultural invention, have not (unless very marginally) interacted with the mainstream of literary creation. Feminist writing is one area where translation now plays this expanded role. Nicole Brossard, for instance, one of Quebec's most important feminist writers, has written extensively on translation and undertaken collaborative 'transform-ance' writing projects. Translators have played an important role in bringing English-Canadian and Quebec writers together – and there are now nascent, although significant, interrelations. This is a totally new occurrence in the history of Canadian letters.

'Translatability' takes on an entirely different meaning now that similar writing traditions exist in the two cultures. In the 1960s, for instance, there was no really obvious solution when translators had to find equivalents for the aggressive intrusion of English into 'joual', Montreal urban slang transformed into a literary language. Untrans-latability was aggressively inscribed in the writing itself; English Canada had produced no equivalent social or literary reality. While many of the feminist texts are difficult to translate because concerned with the very signifying structures of language, these difficulties fall within the questions which writers (within both language groups) are themselves working with. We understand then that the meaning of translatability far exceeds technical concerns and embraces all aspects of the writing context.

Prefaces give us access to the collective dimensions of translatabil-ity, the 'will to knowledge' which creates the need for translations. And in some cases – the Canadian novel is one – they define translation as an activity deeply, and consicously, engaged in the social and political dimensions of literary interchange.

References

Aubert de Gaspé, Philippe (1929) *Philippe, Seigneur d'Haberville*, trans. A. Marquis. Toronto: Musson.

Aubert de Gaspé, Philippe (1974) *Canadians of Old*, trans. Charles G. D. Roberts. Toronto: McClelland and Stewart.

Berman, Antoine (1985) 'La traduction et la lettre', in *Les Tours de Babel. Essais sur la traduction*. Editions Trans-Europ-Repress, Maurezin: 35–150.

Compagnon, Antoine (1979) *La seconde main ou le travail de la citation*. Paris: Editions du Seuil.

Foucault, Michel (1977) 'What Is an Author?', in *Language, Counter-Memory, Practice. Essays and Interviews by Michel Foucault*, ed. D. Bouchard, trans. D. Bouchard and S. Simon. Ithaca, NY: Cornell University Press: 113–38.

Genette, Gérard (1987) *Seuils*. Paris: Editions du Seuil.

Guillerm, Luce (1980) 'L'auteur, les modèles et le pouvoir ou le topique de la traduction au XVIe siècle en France', *Revue des sciences humaines* 52 (180) (Oct.–Dec.): 5–31.

Guillerm, Luce (1984) 'L'intertextualité démontée: le discours sur la traduction', *Littérature* 55 (Oct.): 54–63.

Hazard, Paul (1921) 'L'invasion des littératures du nord dans l'Italie du 18e siècle', *Revue de littérature comparée* 1 (1): 30–67.

Hémon, Louis (1921a) *Maria Chapdelaine*, trans. W. H. Blake. New York: Macmillan.

Hémon, Louis (1921b) *Maria Chapdelaine*, trans. A. McPhail. Montreal: Chapman.

Kirby, William (1884) *Le chien d'or*, trans. L. P. LeMay. Montreal: L'Imprimerie de l'Etendard: v–ix.

Lambert, José (1975) 'La traduction en France à l'époque romantique. A propos d'un article recent', *Revue de littérature comparée* 49 (3) (July–Sept.): 396–412.

Lusignan, Serge (1986) *Parler vulgairement. Les intellectuels et la langue française aux XIIIe et XIVe siècles*. Montreal and Paris: Presses de l'Université de Montréal et Librairie Vrin.

Marie-Victorin, Frère (1925) The Chopping Bee and Other Laurentian Stories, trans. James Ferres. Toronto: Musson: 5.

Ringuet (1940) *Thirty Acres*, trans. Felix and Dorothea Walter. Toronto: Macmillan (preface unpaginated).

Rivard, Adjutor (1924) *Chez Nous: Our Old Quebec Home*, trans. W. H. Blake. Toronto: McClelland and Steward: 16.

Savard, Felix-Antoine (1947) *Boss of the Rivers*, trans Alan Sullivan. Toronto: Ryerson Press: vi.

Simon, Sherry (forthcoming) 'Conflits de juridiction: la double signature du texte traduit', *Meta*.

Staël, Mme Germaine de (1821) 'De l'esprit des traductions', in *Oeuvres complètes*. Paris: 294–7.

12 Translation as Appropriation: The Case of Milan Kundera's *The Joke*

Piotr Kuhiwczak

The word 'appropriation' has only recently become a part of critical discourse, and there are many signs to indicate that all those who promote so-called 'cultural' or 'communication' studies at the expense of humble literary criticism will not let it die. The word which used to describe an act by which one individual was dispossessed by another, without receiving minimal compensation, has been gentrified to such an extent that few academics remember its primary association with the simple and nasty materialistic urge. Thus today's appropriations, linked not to money but to ideas, may be cultural, political, linguistic, spiritual and occasionally even sexual. For many, the term has become a key to a new understanding of the world, since what is history if not a chain of appropriations? What is literature if not an appropriation of one text by another? What is the rise of culture if not a series of appropriations committed by consecutive civilizations? And what is the history of mankind if not an appropriation of women by men – and, it may be said, of men by women?

Indeed, the theory of appropriation is a much more attractive proposition than the ageing theory of progress, which tells us that civilization, despite its temporary lapses, tends toward a final goal – an earthly paradise, a New Jerusalem, or a perfect association of free individuals. It seems, however, that the success of appropriation as a new intellectual concept does not stem so much from its originality as from the fact that it makes everything simple at a time when the theory of progress has been radically undermined.

The theory of appropriation resuscitates a clear vision of reality and a belief in binary oppositions, since it assumes that if there is a gain, there must be a concomitant loss. For these new theoreticians of culture there are no phenomena which escape this polarization, nor are they inclined to accept the simple observation that it would be wise to investigate the nature of appropriation itself, before identifying the victims and the oppressors. Therefore, a substantial part of the scholarship carried on under the umbrella of 'cultural studies' is not devoted to enquiry, but to some kind of intervention on behalf of the supposedly weak, dispossesed and, in one way or another, appropriated. In most cases these are studies of the post-colonial attitudes of Europe and North America towards the Third World, from which one can learn a lot about the author's guilt (especially if s/he lives and works in Western Europe or America), and the author's strong sense of justice; but very little about the problem itself – and next to nothing about its relation to similar problems in the past. The underlying assumption is that, if the theory of appropriation has only recently been articulated, it is because appropriation itself is a relatively recent phenomenon, organically connected with the political and cultural expansion of the major industrial nations. From this assumption it is only a step to the conclusion that appropriation follows on from distorted economic and social relations, and that human nature, unless exposed to such distortions, is incapable of generating both benevolent attitudes and aggressive impulses.

It should be much clearer now why the new theoreticians of culture are not very keen on investigating acts of appropriation in a European context, or learning something from the more or less distant past. Indeed, European history is not gratifying to anyone who likes to pass simple judgements and satisfy an appetite for justice, nor can European appropriations be easily reduced to theoretical paradigms, and lists of gains and losses. Instead, Europe teaches humility, since its history shows that a belief in 'dominant' and 'peripheral' cultures is an illusion, and that sometimes a political or cultural appropriation bears more fruit than a rampant nationalist revival.

If one looks for examples of such complexity, there is none better than that of central Europe – a melting pot of nations, languages, religions and ideologies. There is no form of appropriation to which this part of the world has not been exposed, including physical violence on an unprecedented scale. However, any attempt to assess those events in some theoretical framework fails, since their unique combination contributed to the rise of central European culture – a fascinating mixture of the most refined intellectual values and the most repulsive philosophical and political theories.

The rest of Europe always looked at the space between Germany and Russia with anxiety, if not with a strong sense of bewilderment. Everything there seemed to defeat both a Western and an Eastern European sense of rationality. The small nations quarrelled about their sovereignty, disputed the shapes of borders, launched religious and ideological campaigns and indulged in the suppression of cultural minorities. There is surely more than a grain of truth in the idea that what happened to central Europe in 1945 was less the effect of political calculation than the result of the determined rationality with which the 'three Sages of Yalta' (as Milan Kundera describes the victorious leaders) resolved to put an end to the central European disorder. In her poem 'Voices', the Polish poet Wislawa Szymborska tries to imagine what the 'three Sages of Yalta', and indeed many earlier 'political sages' in Europe, including the Roman emperors, were thinking when they gave their orders:

> These small peoples are thick as flies,
> to the point of irritation,
> satiation and nausea, O Quintus Decius.
>
> One town, another, the hundred and seventieth.
> The stubbornness of the Fidenates. The ill-will of the Faliscans.
> The blindness of the Ecetrans. The vacillation of the Antemnates.
> The studied animosity of the Lavicanians, the Prelignians.
> That's what drives us benevolent men to harshness
> beyond each new hill, O Gaius Cloelius.

And beyond each new border the conquerors saw only darkness:

> Small peoples have small understanding.
> Stupidity surrounds us in an ever-widening circle.
> Objectionable customs. Benighted laws.
> Ineffectual gods, O Titus Vilius.

Thus, in the centre of Europe, the African solution was applied: small peoples were shifted from east to west and from north to south, frontiers were arbitrarily redrawn, new ideological solutions were enthusiastically applied, and cities which already had two names were given a third. Europe seemed to be rationalized at last: the centre had fallen apart, and the East could finally meet the West. The whole enterprise can be seen today not only as an expression of rationality or a manifestation of political will, but also as a major act of translation and appropriation in international relations. The inhabitants of former central Europe had to digest an extremely difficult lesson in both translation and appropriation – but those who witnessed the rise of Eastern Europe were not left unaffected either. For reasons unforeseen by the founding fathers of the new European order, Eastern Europe was a resounding failure as an example of rational cultural and political life. On the one hand it managed to inherit something from its vibrant central European past; on the other, it created its own cultural dynamics – equally distant from the paradigms supplied by the East or by the West. So for the last forty years, Europe has had painstakingly to translate the strange and unpredictable behaviour of 'deplorable small peoples' into familiar codes. In some respects the effects of this lengthy process of translation have been encouraging – the inhabitants of Eastern Europe are no longer regarded as 'deplorable'. At the same time it remains clear that numerous messages have been either missed or misinterpreted, and as a result, the outside world has still very little grasp of some aspects of East European experience.

There is, however, another reason why the new theoreticians of culture do not mind that the interpretation of Eastern Europe has become the domain of professional 'sovietologists', and intellectuals with frustrated political ambitions. For it transpires that any sincerely undertaken intellectual encounter with the former Central or present Eastern Europe is, first and foremost, a taxing personal experience, which only few of us are capable of shaping into an abstract and universally comprehensible form. Such an encounter teaches that even the most horrific and seemingly unimaginable horrors have their origins in the first instance as innocent or noble ideas, and that the distance dividing these ideas from reality can be cut short by a set of circumstances which remain beyond the control of most individuals. There is no doubt that this is not a lesson which can be easily accepted by someone who is used to the idea that ideology, whether 'good' or 'bad', has nothing to do with our personal lives, and therefore it is not at all surprising that so few intellectuals are ready to take on board the thought that a formation of a collective subconscious susceptible to ideological manipulation is only possible when individuals fail to analyse their own actions and moral decisions or find out that an impersonality of the collective or an iron will of the leaders can free them from a burden of personal responsibility.

The puzzled response to literature which comes from the heart of Europe confirms the fact that uncomfortable truths travel with difficulty. And it is by no means the kind of difficulty of which, for instance, the feminist pressure groups speak when they try to market another 'unjustly neglected and seminal' woman novelist of the late eighteenth century.

The apparent passive neglect of Central and East European writing has very little to do with a conspiracy of suppression and calls for no counter-movement. In a well-stocked bookshop of Paris, London or New York, one can always get the novels of Kafka, Singer's short stories, the poetry of Holub or Herbert, and at least one of Mrozek's plays. Nevertheless, most of these writers are regarded as elitist or over-intellectual. The central European writers, unlike, let's say, the Latin American novelists, have never stood a chance of becoming the centre of a publishing 'boom', and with the exception of Kafka, who has been appropriated by German departments all over the world, they have so far been of little concern to tenured academics and aspiring students.

The critical appreciation of East and Central European literature is not a success story either. The abundance of books and articles on Kafka is counterbalanced by the absence, at least in the English-speaking countries, of encouraging accounts of Hasek, Roth, Broch, Schulz and, to a lesser degree, Gombrowicz. The East European postwar writers, who began to be discovered in the 1970s, are occasionally discussed in the columns of review periodicals; it is, however, difficult to get rid of the impression that they are not perceived as writers with something vital to communicate about the human condition, but as political animals, who bring a grim message from 'faraway countries of which we know . . .' only a little more than we did, and whose experience is strictly tangential to that of the 'free world'. There are of course writers – Milosz, for instance – who survive well the onslaught of commercial and political manipulation, and manage to insist that their literature remains literature; but there are also those who choose to compromise like Solzhenitsyn and accept the role of a seasonal attraction in one of the cultural centres of the Western world.

Doubtless some of the writers who eagerly assume the role of *homo politicus* are either sufferers from Byron's disease, or have sensibly realized that their second book will, in any case, be only a lukewarm repetition of the one that gained them recognition. But it is equally true that a genuinely talented writer from Eastern Europe is encouraged in the West to act as something other than a writer. He may well be expected to voice political opinions, in such a way as to please everyone who asks him to speak his mind, and sooner or later he finds out that his works are more often read by politicians than by literary critics, with a view to their politics rather than their literary quality. If he persists in unwillingness to address political issues in a direct way, he will be viewed with increasing suspicion. To resist such enticing 'appropriation' without coming to the conclusion that the freedoms of the West are not less oppressive than the constraints of the East, requires an unusual clarity of mind and an unusual talent.

Milan Kundera is one of those Europeans whose talent goes hand in hand with clarity of mind and strength of character. He is often regarded as one of the greatest living novelists, and his essays on literature and politics are commented on by the leading intellectuals of our time. Kundera's novels can be found on bestseller lists on both sides of the Atlantic, and recently his highly acclaimed work, *The Unbearable Lightness of Being*, has been turned into a film.

In spite of this worldwide recognition, as Kundera has pointed out in numerous interviews, his novels have frequently been misinterpreted, mistranslated, and misunderstood. He even claims that, for some years, he spent more time correcting translations of his novels and chasing the journalists who misrepresented his views than in writing the original works. It would be difficult to measure the effect of this 'close watching' of translators and journalists on the reception of Kundera's works, although he has remarked that of late, the situation has considerably improved. In an interview in 1985 for the American journal *Salmagundi*, he said, 'Initially the media reception proved to be a curse, but I think that today I am read more or less as I should be.'

To an uninformed reader, Kundera's concern with the afterlife of his works might look like a manifestation of unusual conceit or a form of obsession, from which many writers besieged by the media genuinely suffer, but those readers who know the story of the scandal which followed the first English translation of Kundera's early novel *The Joke*, will find the novelist's precautions more than justified.[1]

On the surface, the case of *The Joke* does not look better or worse than many other, less well-documented cases of mistranslation or rewriting. In fact, the history of translation tells us that the appropriation of literary texts by means of rewriting is no novelty, and the mistreatment of Kundera's novel by British, and later on French and American translators, quite pales beside the nineteenth-century French, German, Russian or Polish rewritings of the novels of Scott and Dickens. There is, however, a very significant formal difference between those earlier cases and this of Kundera – namely that *The Joke* was published in a mutilated form long after the literary communities put a stop to 'pirating', by means of universally recognized copyright laws. And this was the basis of Kundera's initial objection when he read the translation of his novel, which appeared in London in 1969. In a letter to *The Times Literary Supplement (TLS)*, he compared the breach of copyright laws by a London publisher to his earlier encounter with a Soviet censor, and arrived at the following conclusion:

In Moscow my play had been altered in good faith that this would help to obtain easy permission to stage it. Neither in Moscow nor in London did anyone care whether I approved the changes or not. The mentality of a London bookseller and that of a Moscow official responsible for art seems to have a mysterious kinship.[2]

What Kundera did not elaborate in his letter from a now 'normalized' Prague was in what way, exactly, the translation differed from the original. He talked about this thirteen years later, in the preface to a completely new translation of *The Joke*. Time had done nothing to moderate his criticism:

The ideologues in Prague took *The Joke* for a pamphlet against socialism and banned it; the foreign publisher took it for a political fantasy that became reality for a few weeks and rewrote it accordingly. (Kundera, 1983: xii)

It is characteristic that in both cases Kundera mentions the Soviet censor and the London publisher in the same breath, as if he wanted to suggest that on the whole, artistic freedom is equally unattainable on either side of the East–West divide.

Indeed, such an interpretation of Kundera has been endorsed by a number of Western intellectuals. Terry Eagleton, for instance, claims in his essay published in *Salmagundi* (1987) that Kundera's 'natural' style subverts the highly artificial, and only recently imposed, ideology of the 'post-capitalist' state, while Western writers have to 'demystify violently' a much more dangerous 'bourgeois' ideology, which 'has had several centuries to disseminate itself into the textures of lived experience, crystallizing its devious impulses as the self-evident or commonsensical.' (Eagleton, 1987). There may be a grain of truth in this undoubtedly novel proposition. The problem is, however, that the subversion of the ideology which Eagleton terms 'post-capitalist', and which both the rulers and the ruled in Eastern Europe call simply 'socialist', is not the main consideration in Kundera's works. The fact that the action of all Kundera's novels is set in postwar Czechoslovakia does not mean that they should be seen as intellectual constructs, aiming to demystify imposed, disseminated or imaginary ideologies. They are actually far more radical – because their main role, as the novelist insists, is to analyse the actions of ordinary people, caught up in situations generated by their own thoughts and their own actions. The fact that some of these thoughts and actions could be termed political only goes to show that political ideas are neither given from above nor created by the so-called masses, but begin and end in the minds of autonomous individuals. Thus what Kundera tells us in both of his comments quoted on the translation of *The Joke*, does not demystify the state of political affairs in either Moscow or London, but simply tells us about some people in these capitals who, through mixing fantasy with reality, took *The Joke* for something which it had never been.

I hope that a closer look at the English text of *The Joke*, and the correspondence which followed its publication in Britain, will help us to realize that the first English version of the novel is not simply an inadequate translation of the Czech text, but an appropriation of the original, resulting from the translators' and publisher's untested assumptions about Eastern Europe, East European writing, and the ability of the Western reader to decode complex cultural messages.

The novel, as Kundera likes to emphasize, is a love story set in Czechoslovakia in the 1950s and 1960s. The main characters – Ludvik, Kostka, Jaroslav and Helena – are at university, at a time when the country is undergoing significant social and political change. The crucial event in the novel is nothing but a joke, which Ludvik plays on his solemn girlfriend Marketa. This joke is simply a postcard in which Ludvik ridicules the official political jargon of the day: 'Optimism is the opium of the people! A healthy atmosphere stinks of stupidity! Long live Trotsky!' But what Ludvik considers funny, the rest of the world sees as serious ideological subversion. So everything that follows from this point of the novel results directly from the fact that none of the characters shares Ludvik's sense of humour. And this is exactly why Ludvik, abandoned by his former friends, is expelled from the university and sent to a penal military unit in Ostrava.

During long years of hard work in Ostrava he falls in love with Lucie. The relationship, very fragile from the start, does not last long, because the girl finds it impossible to reconcile her love for Ludvik, with sexuality. Years after his release, Ludvik goes to his native Moravia where he meets his university colleagues again. The purpose of his trip is to take his revenge on those of them who openly contributed to his banishment from the university. However, the carefully devised and executed plan misfires, because fifteen years after the event nothing is the same: history has thoroughly erased the once-clear line which separated Ludvik's former enemies from his former friends.

I hope that this simplified outline of the novel suffices to demonstrate that its plot is not particularly intricate – typically for Kundera, who insists that the function of the plot in a novel is not to stand on its own, but to serve to develop what he calls 'themes'. He claims that, 'whenever a novel abandons its themes and settles for just telling the story, it goes flat'. This explains why his narratives are so rich and polyphonic, full of seemingly insignificant digressions and carefully crafted repetitions.

For the translators of *The Joke* in 1969, all these structural elements seemed too much of a good thing. As one of them admitted in his letter to the *TLS*, he found the lack of strict chronological order in the book misleading, and even bewildering.[3] With the prospective reader anxiously in mind, he decided to introduce chronology by cutting, 'pasting' and shifting the chapters around. His decision must have been accepted by the publisher, since the editor responsible for the final shape of *The Joke* provided the following justification: 'It is an editor's responsibility to suggest anything that, in his view, might help to clarify things for the reader . . .'.[4]

So the first step in the appropriation of the novel must have been taken on the assumption that narrative forms are not universal but culturally and linguistically specific, therefore their successful translation into another language is a matter of finding forms which would be specific to the culture and language into which a narrative is translated. The translators of *The Joke* assumed then that the main feature which differentiates the Czech narrative forms from the English ones is the lack of strict chronology.

The second major change was introduced into the novel for related reasons. This time, however, it led to the elimination of one of the novel's 'themes'. This might be termed the folk music theme' or, more precisely, the significance of music for the transmission and preservation of cultural tradition. It is introduced when Jaroslav, Vladimir, Helena and Ludvik join a folk music ensemble, and begin to tour the country in the hope that the new 'egalitarian' and 'democratic' society will spontaneously begin to resuscitate and assimilate those ancient folk traditions of Moravia which, according to Marxist theory, had been suppressed and underplayed by bourgeois ideology. The students' initiative wins the full support of the Communist government, which has a policy of promoting any cultural activity that could be interpreted as 'socialist in content and national in form', but in spite of this concerted effort, the masses fail to perceive modernized, socialist folk music as an integral element of their daily lives. Ludvik then realizes, with dismay, that what they do might well be defined as 'socialist content' in 'national form', but that it has nothing to do with genuine folk art. During one of many angry discussions about folk song with Jaroslav, he says: 'You may sing them, you and your ensemble, but show me one other person who does. Show me one collective farmer who sings your collective farm songs for pleasure'. (Kundera, 1983: 134).

And this is the point in the novel at which the earlier passages devoted to the role of Moravian music in the preservation and 'invention' of Czech culture suddenly become meaningful. It is clear, now, that Kundera introduced his long digression on music – Moravian dances, jazz, and the works of Janacek – precisely to illustrate the fragility of culture, and its inherent resistance to any form of conscious or unconscious manipulation.

As in the earlier instance, the translators found the whole theme redundant. What they left in the book was a scattering of general statements, like the following:

The folk song or rite is a tunnel beneath history, a tunnel that keeps alive much of what wars, revolutions, and brutal civilization have long since destroyed above ground, and allows us to look far into the past. (Kundera, 1983: 116)

Deprived of its proper context, the passage sounds like a piece of compressed wisdom from a dictionary of philosophical quotations, leaving no space whatever for doubt. It is possible, however, that the translators believed that only such a 'digested' version of Kundera's thoughts on music could usefully be offered to their readers. This is what one of the translators suggests in his explanatory letter to the *TLS*:

But the vast majority of its English readers as opposed to Czechoslovakian readers with their different cultural traditions, would surely find the chapter on Moravian folk-music with musical examples, if not tedious, at least 'abstruse'.[5]

Reading such justification, one begins to wonder what kind of an operatic performance we could see if the translators of *The Joke* were asked to stage one of Janacek's operas?

Apart from these major alterations, there are a number of less conspicuous intrusions into the text of the novel. The fact that these changes are comparatively minor does not make them insignificant to the overall structure of the book. In some cases, in fact, they strip whole layers of meaning from the narrative, and leave only what the author of *The Joke* calls a 'flat' story. The best illustration of what these seemingly minor adjustments do to the novel is Part Five (according to the 1983 edition), in which Ludvik is trying to make sense of Lucie's behaviour. He asks himself a question about the significance of his actions:

Do love stories, apart from happening, being, have something to say? For all my scepticism, I had clung to a few superstitions – the strange conviction, for example, that everything in life that happens to me has a sense beyond itself, *means* something, that life in its day-to-day events speaks to us about itself, that it gradually reveals a secret, that it takes the form of a rebus whose message must be deciphered, that the stories we live in comprise the mythology of our lives and in that mythology lies the key to truth and mystery. Is it all an illusion? Possibly, even probably, but I can't seem to rid myself of the need to *decipher* my life continually. (Kundera, 1983: 140)

In a way this paragraph, so lightheartedly removed from the 1969 edition, sums up the main theme of the novel – Ludvik's quest for rational patterns in life despite his discovery that anything which happens to him takes him by surprise. In fact, the never-ending exploration of life's possibilities is Kundera's artistic obsession, and the novel itself, he believes, is 'a meditation on existence as seen through the medium of imaginary characters'. If this principal element of his writing is either missed or consciously rejected – and this is what happened in the 1969 translation – the novels lose their universal appeal, and the remaining structures suspended in a vacuum, require a new binding contextualization. The truth is, however, that in most cases such a new contextualization distorts and reduces the original work instead of simplifying it in a positive way. The new contextualization of *The Joke* reminds us again that only an artistically complex literary work is capable of investigating potentially complex existential situations. The Italian writer Primo Levi, who recognized simplification as a useful cognitive faculty, warned against its excessive use:

This *desire* for simplification is justified, but the same does not always apply to simplification itself. It is a working hypothesis, useful so long as it is recognised as such and not mistaken for reality; the greater part of historical and natural phenomena is not simple, or not simple with the simplicity we would like. (Levi, 1988: 23; emphasis in original)

I hope I have shown clearly that the translators of *The Joke* have trespassed across the magical line beyond which simplification can be taken for reality. What remains unexplained is the question of where they should have stopped in their attempt to make the book simple for the reader. The very fact that Kundera forced the publishers to bring out the complete version of the novel in 1970, and then requested a new translation which appeared thirteen years later, tells us that the damage was beyond repair. But there is actually objective and reliable evidence that *The Joke* did not need any simplification in the first place. It is the response of its readers, who turned out to be much more perceptive than the translators initially assumed. One, who joined the debate in the *TLS*, compared the translation with the Czech original and reached the following conclusion:

I cannot judge the translation, though I am puzzled to learn that parts of the original would have been 'abstruse' to readers here. I read the original and found it easy to follow.[6]

But more evidence comes from those who did not read Czech and had to rely for their judgement on the English text. What this evidence amounts to is a collection of critical statements, which apart from reflecting the mistaken assumptions of the translators, tell us something about convictions and prejudices with which the reviewers approached Kundera's book.

The most common impression produced by the translation was that the novel, in spite of its artistic merit, was not about human experience in general, but about human experience in a particular historical context. At their best the critics hesitated, and tried to make out whether they were dealing with the particular or the universal. The *TLS* reviewer, for instance, went out of his way to stress that 'the novel reflects, even in local details, aspects of growing up in Britain during the same period – this, despite the fact that so much of the 'local detail' had been removed from the text.[7] However, his initial enthusiasm over its familiarity is undercut in the concluding paragraph, where he decides that 'the novel could only have been written in a society where Marxism had been taken seriously'. Thus we obtain from this review the impression that life is the same everywhere, but in order to realize the fact, we should live in a society which takes Marxism seriously. Today, we may laugh and toss this piece of writing aside, but should we blame the reviewer for the officiousness of the translator?

The unfortunate story of *The Joke* was finally brought to a happy conclusion. A revised edition of the novel was published in 1970, and the 1969 version was withdrawn from the market and most libraries. In 1983 a translation approved by the author and made by Michael H. Heim appeared in Britain and the United States.

But apart from everything else there is an ironic aspect to this story which convinces us that the road to hell is truly paved with good intentions. When one of the translators confessed in his apologetic letter, 'I read the book and fell in love with it to such an extent, indeed, that while I was working on it I managed to read most of it aloud to my wife over ironing and the like'[8] – he did not realize how ominous a confession it was. For Kundera, whose novels explore the ambiguity of human feelings, there is nothing more abhorrent than the presumptuousness which may lurk in possessive maternal love, which in good faith stifles and alters the object of its feeling, in much the same way as the translator stifled and altered *The Joke*.

The remaining novels by Kundera had much better luck with their translators, most of whom obtained his stamp of approval. We cannot be sure whether it is the high quality of these translations which has stimulated the general interest in Kundera's works in the last decade in Britain and elsewhere; but it is clear that there are readers with sufficient taste and intelligence to cope happily with the complexities of Kundera's novels, and who do not need to resort to culturally simplified editions.

What remains puzzling, however, is the fact that Kundera's popularity with readers stands in reverse proportion to his popularity with British literary critics. Apart from an illuminating book by Robert Porter (1981) there has been little written about him that one would wish to read, or could recommend to students. As the recent crop of publicity following the screening of *The Unbearable Lightness of Being* shows, Kundera, in spite of his optimism, is still in the grip of flourishing appropriation. His novels are constantly being taken for what they are not – political fantasy, or diatribes against Eastern European reality.

The Canadian writer François Ricard believes it is the 'dangerous' character of Kundera's writing which either frightens some critics or makes them confine their analyses to the realm of Kundera's dissidence:

Despite its innocent appearance, Milan Kundera's work is one of the most *demanding* we have been given to read today, and I use the word *demanding* in its most radical sense, to mean that this work presents a challenge to the mind and the heart that is extremely difficult to take up. To accept it, to consent truly to it is to risk being swept much further away than one had at first believed, to the very limit of consciousness, to that 'ravaged galaxy' where the hero of *The Joke* finds himself at the end of the novel. (Ricard, 1987: 58)

Thus, unlike many so called 'post-modernist' Western European writers, Kundera and some other contemporary Central Europeans are deceptively serious in their playfulness. And since their works are so uncompromising and invite a 'take it or leave it' response, maybe it is understandable if some of us accept the latter option and follow Gabriel Josipovici who, in his recent review of *The Art of the Novel*, 'left' Kundera and opted instead for the safety of Robbe-Grillet, Perec and Nabokov:

One does not have to adhere to the norms of the nineteenth-century novel to feel that there are many other, as yet unrealized, possibilities in the form, and that quite a few are realized in ways very different from Kundera's in the novels of, say, Robbe-Grillet, Georges Perec, Nabokov, Sciascia and Appelfeld. (Josipovici, 1988: 696)

Notes

1. *The Joke* (*Zert*) was originally published in Czechoslovakia in 1967 by Verlag Československy Spesovatel. The first English translation by David Hamblyn and Oliver Stallybrass was published in 1969 by Macdonald & Co. (Publishers) Ltd, London. The edition in which the omitted passages were reinstated appeared in 1970 as the Penguin Books hardcover edition. In 1983 Faber and Faber published the new American translation of *The Joke* by Michael Henry Heim.
2. *The Times Literary Supplement*, 30 October 1969: 1256.
3. Ibid., 6 November 1969: 1283.
4. Ibid.: 1282.
5. Ibid., 20 November 1969: 1339.
6. Letter from H. G. Alexander. *The Times Literary Supplement*, 13 November 1969: 1312.
7. 'Behind the Masks', *The Times Literary Supplement*, 12 October 1969: 1122.
8. *The Times Literary Supplement*, 6 November 1969: 1283.

References

Eagleton, Terry (1987) 'Estrangement and Irony', *Salmagundi* 73: 25–33.
Josipovici, Gabriel (1988) 'The Ironist Aloof', *The Times Literary Supplement* 24–30 June: 695–6.
Kundera, Milan (1983) 'Author's Preface', in *The Joke*. London: Faber and Faber.
Levi, Primo (1988) *The Drowned and the Saved*, trans. Raymond Rosenthal. London: Michael Joseph.
Porter, R. (1981) *Milan Kundera: A Voice from Central Europe*, Aarhus, Arkoha.
Ricard, François (1987) 'Satan's Point of View', *Salmagundi* 73: 58.

Index